THE ARMENIAN VERSION

OF THE

TESTAMENT OF JOSEPH

SOCIETY OF BIBLICAL LITERATURE

TEXTS AND TRANSLATIONS SERIES

PSEUDEPIGRAPHA SERIES

edited by

Robert A. Kraft

TEXTS AND TRANSLATIONS 6

PSEUDEPIGRAPHA SERIES
5

THE ARMENIAN VERSION

OF THE

TESTAMENT OF JOSEPH

SCHOLARS PRESS
Missoula, Montana

THE ARMENIAN VERSION

OF THE

TESTAMENT OF JOSEPH

Introduction,

Critical Edition, and Translation

by

Michael E. Stone

Published by

SCHOLARS PRESS

for

The Society of Biblical Literature

Distributed by

SCHOLARS PRESS
University of Montana
Missoula, Montana 59801

THE ARMENIAN VERSION

OF THE

TESTAMENT OF JOSEPH

Introduction,

Critical Edition, and Translation

by

Michael E. Stone

Library of Congress Cataloging in Publication Data

Bible. O. T. Apocryphal books. Testaments of the twelve
   patriarchs. Joseph. Armenian. 1975.
   The Armenian version of the Testament of Joseph.

   (Pseudepigrapha series ; 5)   (Texts and translations ; 6)
   Bibliography: p.
   I. Stone, Michael E., 1938-   II. Bible. O. T.
Apocryphal books. Testaments of the twelve patriarchs.
Joseph. English. Stone. 1975. III. Bible. O. T.
Apocryphal books. Testaments of the twelve patriarchs.
Armenian. 1975. IV. Title. V. Series. VI. Series:
Society of Biblical Literature. Texts and translations ;
6.
BS1830.T4A75 1975   229'.914   75-29210
ISBN 0-89130-035-X

Copyright © 1975

by

The Society of Biblical Literature

Printed in the United States of America
1 2 3 4 5 6
Printing Department
University of Montana
Missoula, Montana 59801

PREFACE TO THE SERIES

TEXTS AND TRANSLATIONS is a project of the Committee on Research and Publications of the Society of Biblical Literature and is under the general direction of George W. MacRae (Harvard Divinity School), Executive Secretary and Harry M. Orlinsky (Hebrew Union College-Jewish Institute of Religion, New York), Chairman of the Committee. The purpose of the project is to make available in convenient and inexpensive format ancient texts which are not easily accessible but are of importance to scholars and students of "biblical literature" as broadly defined by the Society. Reliable modern English translations will accompany the texts. Occasionally the various series will include documents not published elsewhere. It is not a primary aim of these publications to provide authoritative new critical texts, nor to furnish extensive annotations. The editions are regarded as provisional, and individual volumes may be replaced in the future as better textual evidence becomes available. The following subseries have been established thus far:

PSEUDEPIGRAPHA, edited by Robert A. Kraft (University of Pennsylvania)

GRECO-ROMAN RELIGION, edited by Hans Dieter Betz (School of Theology at Claremont)

EARLY CHRISTIAN LITERATURE, edited by Birger A. Pearson (University of California at Santa Barbara)

For the PSEUDEPIGRAPHA SERIES the choice of texts is governed in part by the research interests of the SBL Pseudepigrapha Group, of which George W.E. Nickelsburg, Jr. (University of Iowa) is currently Chairman and James H. Charlesworth (Duke University) Secretary. This series will focus on Jewish materials from the Hellenistic era and will regularly include volumes that incorporate the fragmentary evidence of works attributed to biblical personalities, culled from a wide range of Jewish and Christian sources. The volumes are selected, prepared, and edited in consultation with the following editorial subcommittee of the Pseudepigrapha Group:

Sebastian P. Brock (Cambridge University, England)

George W. MacRae (Harvard Divinity School)

George W.E. Nickelsburg, Jr. (University of Iowa)

Michael E. Stone (Hebrew University, Israel)

John Strugnell (Harvard Divinity School)

Robert A. Kraft, Editor

v

TABLE OF CONTENTS

PREFACE   1

INTRODUCTION   3

    Previous Editions and Studies   3

    The Present Edition and the Manuscripts   4

    The Text   7

    The Apparatus   9

    The Translation   10

    Critical Signs and Abbreviations   11

    List of Manuscripts Cited   12

TEXT, TRANSLATION, APPARATUS   14

PREFACE

The edition of the Testament of Joseph presented here would not have been achieved without the encouragement and help of a number of friends and colleagues. The manuscripts were made available, most generously, by the various libraries concerned, the Armenian Patriarchate in Jerusalem, the Mechitarist Fathers in Venice, the Nationalbibliothek in Vienna, and the Matenadaran in Erevan. A. Hultgård in Lund and M. van Esbroeck in Brussels had a part in preparing collations of some of the samples.

M. de Jonge of Leiden has encouraged me in this project, and in the broader labour of the preparation of an edition of all of the Testaments. To him and his co-workers I owe a special debt.

G.W.E. Nickelsburg of the Pseudepigrapha Group of the Society for Biblical Literature has been a continued support and a good friend. His help both in moral encouragement and in the material preparation of the English part of the final typescript is gratefully acknowledged. To the Group itself is due the stimulus which brought about the preparation of this edition. My research into the Testaments of the Twelve Patriarchs has been supported at various times by the Research Funds of the Hebrew University and by the Israel Academy of Sciences and Humanities. To all these and others, thanks are given.

Jerusalem
June 16, 1975

INTRODUCTION

Recent years have seen an arousal of interest in the textual study of the Pseudepigrapha in general and of their Oriental versions in particular. It is within this general context that this edition of the Armenian version of the Testament of Joseph is presented. The nature of the series in which it is published requires the introduction to be indicative rather than exhaustive. It sets before the reader the past history of publication of this text and the principles according to which this edition has been prepared. The detailed analysis of the relationship between the manuscripts and their families is not given here, but its chief results are set forth. They can be verified by recourse to the textual material presented.

Previous Editions and Studies

The chief previous publications of part or all of the text of the Armenian version of the Testaments of the Twelve Patriarchs are the following:[1]

1. The Testaments of Reuben, Simeon and Levi from the Calcutta manuscript were printed in the Armenian periodical *Azkaser Araratean* 3 (Calcutta: 1850), pp. 446-448, 454-456, 469-472, 478-480. See no. 5 below.

2. Brief extracts from the Testament of Joseph were published by N. Marr in *Handes Amsorya* 5 (1891), pp. 260-271,[2] and further extracts in *Sborniki pritč Vardana. Materialy dlja istorii srednevěkovoj armjanskoj literatury*, III (St. Petersburg: 1894), pp. 61 f. (*non vidi*).

3. The text of all the Testaments of the Twelve Patriarchs was published by S. Yovsēp'ianc', *Ankanon Girk' Hin Ktakaranac'* (Venice: 1896), pp. 27-151. His edition is based on Venice, Mechitarist 280, with nos. 346, 679, 229, and 1270 of that library also consulted.

4. Some readings from additional manuscripts were included, mainly in Greek retroversion, in the apparatus of R.H. Charles, *The Greek Versions of the Testaments of the XII Patriarchs* (Oxford: 1908), but his information is not reliable.

5. The Testament of Levi was published on the basis of eight manuscripts belonging to the Armenian Patriarchate in Jerusalem by M.E. Stone, *The Testament of Levi* (Jerusalem : 1969). This volume also includes a republication of no. 1 as well as all the variant readings in nos. 3 and 4. The

---

[1] In greater detail see Ch. Burchard, no. 7, below; Stone, no. 5 below. (The numbers in this and the following notes refer to the bibliographical list in this section.)

[2] Also in Russian, see Burchard, no. 7 below, pp. 12 ff.

3

manuscripts used were Jerusalem, Armenian Patriarchate 1925 (siglum M), 428, 501, 1927, 1933, 1934, 939, and 1170.

6. Further samples from the Testaments of Zebulun, Joseph and Benjamin based on the same manuscripts were published in: M.E. Stone, 'The Jerusalem Manuscripts of the Testaments of the Twelve Patriarchs: Samples of Text,' *Sion* 44 (1970), pp. 29-35.

The following recent studies relating to the Armenian version of the Testaments of the Twelve Patriarchs should also be noted:

7. Ch. Burchard, 'Zur armenischen Ueberlieferung der Testamente der Zwölf Patriarchen,' *Studien zu den Testamenten der Zwölf Patriarchen*, ed. W. Eltester (BZNW 38; Berlin: 1969), pp. 1-29. This is an extremely useful analysis and assembly of all material relating to the version known at that time. See also review in *JBL* 89 (1970), pp. 487 f.

8. A. Hultgård, *Croyances messianiques des Test. XII Patr.* (dissertation; Uppsala: 1971), pp. 22-37.

9. M.E. Stone, 'Methodological Issues in the Study of the Text of the Apocrypha and Pseudepigrapha,' *Proceedings of the Fifth World Congress of Jewish Studies*, I (Jerusalem: 1971), pp. 213-217.

10. M.E. Stone, 'The Jerusalem Manuscripts of the Testaments of the Twelve Patriarchs: Selection of Manuscripts,' *Sion* 49 (1975) forthcoming.

11. M. de Jonge, 'The Greek Testaments of the Twelve Patriarchs and the Armenian Version,' *Studies on the Testaments of the Twelve Patriarchs. Text and Interpretation* ('Studia in V.T. Pseudepig., III ; Leiden: 1975) forthcoming.

The Present Edition and the Manuscripts

The edition of the Armenian version of the Testament of Joseph published here represents an advance over all previous editions as it is based on new collations of a carefully selected group of manuscripts. The procedures by which the numerous manuscripts were evaluated and this group of manuscripts selected have been expounded in detail elsewhere.[3]

It is well, however, here to recapitulate them briefly. Samples of the text of the Testaments of the Twelve Patriarchs were selected. These were T. Levi chs. 1, 8, 19, T. Zebulun ch. 9, T. Joseph ch. 19, and T. Benjamin chs. 11-12. The text of these examples was examined in all accessible Armenian manuscripts, twenty-nine of the fifty-two known manuscripts being collated thus against an agreed basis, Jerusalem, Armenian Patriarchate 1925. Among these manuscripts were all those written before the seventeenth century and a considerable number of those written in that century.[4]

---

[3] See details in Stone, nos. 6 and 9.

[4] See details in Stone, no. 10.

From among the numerous variants found in these manuscripts those cases were isolated in which a reading present in half or less of them agreed with the Greek text, with a variant to the Greek text, or was insubitably superior to the other Armenian readings.[5] Such readings (including a number of apparent splits in the tradition) occurred in four textual families: a) the 'short' recension (*alpha*), and three different 'long' text forms; b) Erevan, Matenadaran 1500; c) Jerusalem, Armenian Patriarchate 1925, and Erevan, Matenadaran, 353; and d) the text form called, since Charles' day, *beta,* to which all the other 'long' text manuscripts belong.[6]

Family alpha

Six manuscripts of this family were available for study. From the samples it is clear that three of them, if utilized, contain all possibly original readings of this recension.[7] These manuscripts are:

K   Vienna, Mechitarist 128, 1388 C.E.

S   Jerusalem, Armenian Patriarchate 939, 1621, C.E.

W   Vienna, Mechitarist 705, 1403 C.E.

In addition one further manuscript was consulted in cases where part of *alpha* alone seems to preserve an original reading:

B   Venice, Mechitarist 679, 15th century.

This form of the text has definitely undergone recensional activity, but it has as its base, a textual form of very high value. Cases where *alpha* alone or *alpha* with one of the better forms of the 'long' text preserves a superior reading are quite frequent.[8] The six manuscripts of *alpha* examined separate into three subgroups, K H (Bodleian Arm e 30); B W ; and A (Venice, Mechitarist 346) S. These groups are, however, conflate among themselves and show conflate readings with the various forms of the long text. Manuscript W in the present work will be seen to show many expansionary readings.

---

[5]M. de Jonge graciously put copies of the new collations of the Greek manuscripts at our disposal. These were prepared by him and his associates in Leiden and were available both for the samples and for the whole of the Testament of Joseph.

[6]See Stone, no. 10, Appendix I.

[7]*Ibid*, Appendix II.

[8]Examples to demonstrate this and the following evaluations are adduced in Stone, no. 10. Cases of splits in the Armenian tradition where both Armenian readings occur in Greek are found, but require separate study. They are not listed here.

Family Z

Z   Erevan, Matenadaran 1500, 1282-83 C.E.

This manuscript contains a unique text form, the best preserved text. It serves as the base text for the present edition. In spite of its general superiority, there are a number of cases in which another family or families preserved an indubitably superior reading. Such have been listed below.

Family MV

M   Jerusalem, Armenian Patriarchate 1925, 1269 C.E.

V   Erevan, Matenadaran 353, 1317 C.E.

These two manuscripts were found in the samples (Stone, no. 10) to contain a text occasionally superior to Z and often superior to *alpha* and *beta*. Now, the examination of a considerable body of text, the whole of the Testament of Joseph, has enabled a greater measure of precision in the establishment of the relationship between these manuscripts. Neither is a copy of the other and M is generally closer to the archetype. The unique readings of V are in virtually all cases corruptions or inferior readings. Only in cases where M stands alone is V superior to it. It follows, therefore, that V need only be cited or consulted in cases in which M stands alone. This principle has been followed in the edition.

Family <u>beta</u>

This family, which encompasses the great majority of Armenian manuscripts of the Testaments of the Twelve Patriarchs, is also, given the survival of families Z and MV, the least important from the point of view of restoration of the original text of the version. Three manuscripts were selected on the basis of the samples to represent this family in the present edition (See Stone, no. 10). These are divided into two types:

L   Vienna, Nationalbibl. Arm. 11, before 1608 C.E.

This manuscript is close to the main body of manuscripts of *beta*, but in the samples it contained a few readings indicating a measure of independence, and perhaps superiority to the rest of the manuscripts of *beta*.

X   Erevan, Matenadaran 346, 1390 and 1400 C.E.

Bb   Venice, Mechitarist 280, 1418-1422 C.E.

These two manuscripts form a distinct subgroup of *beta*. Bb is the manuscript used by Yovsēp'ianc' (no. 3 above) and previously designated B*. This subgroup is reworked and expansionary, but contains a number of readings which may be primitive. As was the case for V, so too here the examination of a larger body of text than in the samples indicates that the unique readings of Bb preserve nothing superior to X or the other witnesses. Thus it is only cited in the apparatus where the reading of X is of particular interest or importance.

The Text

The text is based on Z except in cases where other families preserve superior readings. Such superior readings are overwhelmingly cases of agreement with the Greek text. The following list records all cases where the reading of a family other than Z has been accepted into the text.

1:1 his 2°]   om   Z X K
1:2 my sons and my brothers]   M V   variants of this   K S W   om rel
1:4 my fathers]   our fathers   Z W
1:6 I was 2°]   om   Z S W
1:7 calumnies]   evils   Z
2:2 my father]   my fathers Z
τοῦ πατρός μου majority Greek with variant τῶν πατέρων μου in *l c*. Word order in Armenian = majority Greek, while that in *l* varies and *c* om Israel. It might, however, be maintained that Z should be preferred by *lectio difficilior*. *Non liquet*.
2:4 Lord]   om M L   *after* him Z :   majority Armenian = Greek *var. lect.*
2:6 the thought of the soul]   the thoughts of the souls   Z
3:3 I prayed]   praying Z :   not equivalent to Greek *h*
3:5 them]   om   Z K
     the sick]   I was sick Z :   corrupt
3:8 wished to drag...along]   summoned Z   wished to cast   K S W
4:2 in]   om   Z S :   corrupt
     is]   om   Z
4:5 you wish]   I wish   Z   I will wish   K
4:6 to her]   om   Z
4:8 I continued]   *after* pray   Z
6:2 and 1°]   it was   Z
6:4 food 1°]   M L   foods   rel
     food 2°]   M K   foods   rel.
6:6 to me]   X K S B   thing (*corruption of* to me)   Bb   om rel
7:5 your rival]   K S* W   om Z   your son's rival   rel
7:7 thus]   M X L W   this   rel
     Arm rel does not correspond to Greek *d* αὐτά
9:1 and said]   K S W   om   rel
10:4 work]   M K   words   rel
     thought]   M X K W   thoughts   rel
     a man might transgress]   M K S W I   transgress   Z
     you might be in need   X   you might transgress   L

11:1   brothers]   + and   Z
12:3   against him]   om   Z   against them   X
13:1   commanded to bring]   W B   brought   X L   brings   rel
13:4   to be---naked]   to undress him and to torture (him)   Z

   Compare, however, Z with Greek *d* in 13:9, indicating that
   the textual situation may be more complex than is evident
   at first sight.

13:8   did you become]   are you   Z
14:2   he said]   X Bb   om rel.

   This may be a split, since φησίν is omitted by *dl a ch*.

14:3   he who was stolen]   those who were stolen   Z M

   Cf. Greek vs. 1.

15:2   of yourself]   om   Z   to us   X L
17:7   soul ... soul]   field ... field   Z
18:1   he will glorify]   they will glorify   Z

   he will exalt]   they will exalt   Z M*

18:3   them]   him (*or* her)   Z K
19:12 will come to an end]   K S W   will be at the end   Z M
       will be an end   X L
20:3   and by---mother 2°]   om   Z

   In addition to these cases, the following readings have
not been incorporated into the text, although it seems likely
(but not certain) that they are primitive:

9:5   to make me stumble   K S
10:5   now]   Z   om rel.   The reading of Z may be secondary.

   Greek presents only γάρ in *d m*.

13:4   he 3°]   *Petap'rē*   W B.

   This may be original and apparently parallels the un-
   animous reading of Greek. However, W B also add the
   proper name instead of "he 1°" in this same verse where
   it has no Greek support. This may indicate a tendency
   of these manuscripts.

14:3   these]   your   K S W

   for you will   X L S W

   These two readings concord with the Greek of vs. 1, which
   is apparently common, in part, with Armenian vs. 3.
   Since the difference between the versions is considerable,
   however, it is wisest to suspend judgement.

16:2   again]   om X L W.

   The word may be additional in Armenian and has no Greek
   support.

17:5   me]   Z   om rel.   See preceding comment.

18:1 for ever   X L.

> This is undoubtedly a primitive reading. The order of the two verbs is different in Armenian and Greek, and so the occurrence of this adverb with the verb 'he will exalt' in X L is not original. It should perhaps be read with the preceding 'glorify', but the history of the text is not certain enough to include this reading in the text of the edition.

Apart from these cases, the text of Z is reproduced exactly except for a standardization of spelling and punctuation. This manuscript displays certain orthographic peculiarities which have been changed without any notice being given in the text or apparatus.

The diphthong *ea* is always written as *e* by the manuscript.

The long vowel *ē* is never found in the manuscript, only *e*.

The manuscript never writes the final *-y* in endings *-ay*, *-oy* unless they are followed by a demonstrative.

The manuscript never writes *-y-* in triphthongs *-ayi*, *-aye-*, etc.

The manuscript always writes *w* for *ow* when followed by a vowel.

The manuscript always has the spellings *važjan* for *vaxčan*, *ĕndrem* for *ĕntrem* and so in other derivatives, *hrštak* for *hreštak*.

All these cases have been standardized. All abbreviations have been resolved, including numerals. Chapter and verse division have been introduced following the Greek version. No verse or section division is indicated in the manuscript.

The Apparatus

The apparatus presents all variants of possible significance for the study of the substantive readings preserved by the manuscripts. It is not exhaustive of all variants existing between the manuscripts, and the following classes of variants, being chiefly of orthographic and scribal character, have been excluded:

1) standard spelling alternations such as *aw/ō*, *e/ē*; otiose *i* found particularly in M V preceding words, commencing with a vowel, to which the inseparatable form of this preposition (*y-*) has already been prefixed; simple spelling variants and errors of spelling.

In addition certain classes of 'Repetitive Variants' (see Stone, no. 5, pp. 197-198) have been excluded from the apparatus. Such are:

2) case variation in possessive pronouns and adjectives, such as *im/imum*, *jerum/jeroy*, etc.; tense variation in verbs except where likely to reflect a Greek original, such as variants *asē/asēr/asac'* in narrative contexts or present and aorist subjunctive in a future sense; addition or omission of demonstrative *-s/ -t/ -n* and variations between these and their analogues *ays*, *ayt*, *ayn*, etc. and compounds thereof; addition or omission of *i* following verbs of becoming or preceding infinitives expressing purpose or result; simple morphological

alternatives like *koč'ec'eal/ koč'eal*; the addition or omission of *t'e* or *et'e* before direct speech and variation between these two forms; addition or omission of personal pronouns with conjugated forms of the verb unless reflecting extant Greek readings; minor variants of word order; variations of synonyms *ibrew/orpēs, yoržam/ibrew, amenayni/amenec'un, kam/ew kam* in lists.

In addition, for the sake of simplicity, simple spelling practice has been standardized throughout the apparatus. *aw* is always written not *ō*, in spite of the practice of the later manuscripts, and the usage of *ē* conforms to that in the text.

The Translation

The translation is as literal as normal English usage will permit. Any words introduced by the editor and the editor's emendations of the text are surrounded by parentheses. The apparatus has been translated into English, although not all the variants were amenable to translation. All variants involving a change in the meaning of the text have been included, as well as many others. The English translation of the apparatus incorporates a small number of editor's comments, alternative translations, and the like. The aim of this English rendering of the apparatus is to provide students of the Greek text with access to a large portion of the variant readings of the Armenian manuscripts. It is natural that the vast majority of variant readings so translated are of inner-Armenian origin. In Armenian their genesis is often obvious. This is not so in English, and to explain each case would require the addition of a major commentary, an undertaking quite beyond the scope of this edition.

CRITICAL SIGNS AND ABBREVIATIONS

⟨ ⟩	editor's emendation of the text
( )	editor's emendation of or addition to the translation
+	adds
1°, 2°, 3°, etc.	following a word indicates the first, second, third, etc. occurrence of the word in the verse
A*, B*, C*, etc.	the text as written by the original scribe
A°, B°, C°, etc.	the text as corrected by the original scribe
A^c, B^c, C^c, etc.	the text as corrected by an unidentified hand other than the original scribe
word---word	indicates all words between the two words so linked
word...word	indicates only those two words so linked
ante	before
ed	editor
eras	erasure
fin	end of verse
inc	start of verse
lit.	literally
om	omits
omn	all manuscripts
plur.	plural
post	after
praepon	places in front of
rel	all manuscripts except those quoted explicitly by siglum
sing.	singular

LIST OF MANUSCRIPTS CITED

B	Venice, Mechitarist 705, 1403 C.E.	pp. 40-53
K	Vienna, Mechitarist 128, 1388 C.E.	fols. 121v-135v
L	Vienna, Nationalbibl. Arm. 11, before 1608 C.E.	fols. 538v-539v
M	Jerusalem, Armenian Patriarchate 1925, 1269 C.E.	pp. 508-512
S	Jerusalem, Armenian Patriarchate 939, 1621 C.E.	pp. 214-225
V	Erevan, Matenadaran 353, 1317, C.E.	fols. 658v-660v
W	Vienna, Mechitarist 705, 1403 C.E.	fols. 208r-212r
X	Erevan, Matenadaran 346, 1390-1400 C.E.	fols. 33v-35r
Z	Erevan, Matenadaran 1500, 1282-83 C.E.	fols. 238r-239r
Bb	Venice, Mechitarist 280, 1418-1422 C.E.	fols. 141r-143v

ERRATA IN THE APPARATUS

3:6, line 3, read "եզիպտացւոյն] Z -ոչոյն rel"

6:1, preceding "եւ] Z ..."read " առաբեաց] արձակեաց K արձակէր W :

8:1, line 5: "փախեայ] ..."read "գչանդերձն իմ եւ X:

THE TESTAMENT OF JOSEPH

TEXT, TRANSLATION, APPARATUS

ԿՏԱԿ ՅՈՎՍԵՓԱՅ ՎԱՍՆ ՆԱԽԱՆՁՈՒ

1:1 Հրաման կտակի Յովսեփայ յորժամ հանդերձեալ էր վախճանել։ Կոչեաց զորդիս իւր եւ զեղբարս իւր եւ ասէ ցնոսա. 2 Որդեակք իմ եւ եղբարք իմ, լուարուք Յովսեփայ սիրեցելոյս յիսրայէլէ, եւ ունկնդիք որդիք իմ հալրս ձերում։ 3 Ես տեսի ի կեանս իմում գնախանձ եւ զմահ, եւ ոչ մոլորեցայ ի ճշմարտութենէն Տեառն. 4 Եղբարք իմ այսքիկ ատեցին զիս, եւ Տէր սիրեաց զիս, սոքա կամէին սպանանել զիս, եւ Աստուած հարցն իմոց պահեաց զիս. ի ջրհոր ընկեցին զիս, եւ Բարձրեալն եհան զիս. 5 ի ծառայութիւն վաճառեցայ, եւ Տէրն ամենացուն ազատեաց զիս. ի գերութիւն վարեցայ, եւ հզաւր ձեռն նորա աւգնեաց ինձ. սովով պաշարեցայ, եւ նոյն ինքն Տէրն դարմանեաց զիս. 6 Մ՛իայն եի եւ Աստուած մխիթարեաց զիս. ի հիւանդութեան եի, եւ Բարձրեալն այցելու եղեւ ինձ. ի

կտակք S : + եղբարցն L

1:1 կտակի] պատասխանեաց M L   + պատասխանւոյ (-լոյն X) X W+ պատասխանեացն K :   կոչեաց] կոչեալ M V :   զեղբարսն իւր եւ զորդիսն X :   իւր 1°] om S W :   իւր 2°] om Z X K

2 որդեակք---իմ 2°] M V   եղբ. իմ եւ որդ. K S եղբ. իմ եւ որդ. իմ W   om rel :   յիսրայէլէ] + հալր ձերոյ X :   որդիք---ձերում] բանից իմոց X :   որդիք իմ] om S : իմ 3°] om K W

3 զմահ] + եւ ոչ նախանձեցայ K

4 inc] Z W   + եւ rel :   իմ] om L :   զիս 1°--- զիս 2°] om X L :   սոքա] եւ X :   եւ 2°] այլ S :   իմոց] մերոց Z W :   պահեաց] ապրեցոյց K

5 եւ 1°---վարեցայ] om W S* :   տէր 1°---տէր 2°] om K :   ի գեր. վարեցայ] om S :   վարեցայ] վաճառեցայ M : եւ հզաւր---պաշարեցայ] om X L :   հզաւր ձեռն] ձեռն հալր S հալր ձեռն W :   նոյն] Z post   տէրն M   om rel

6 աստուած] + հալր իմոյ X :   եի 2°] է L om Z S W : եւ 2°] om S W :   բարձրեալն 1°] աստուած M L K S W

THE TESTAMENT OF JOSEPH CONCERNING ENVY

1:1 The instruction of the testament of Joseph when he was about to die. He summoned his sons and his brothers and said to them, 2 "My sons and my brothers, listen to Joseph beloved by Israel and attend, my sons, to your father. 3 I saw envy and death during my life and I did not stray from the Lord's truth. 4 These brothers of mine hated me and the Lord loved me, they desired to kill me and the God of my fathers preserved me, they cast me into a well and the Most High drew me forth. 5 I was sold into slavery and the Lord of all freed me, I was led into captivity and his mighty hand aided me, I was beset by hunger and the same Lord himself nurtured me. 6 I was alone and God comforted me, I was in sickness and the Most High was my visitor, in prison and

---

Testaments S :   + of the brothers L

    1:1 of the testament]   of replies M L   + of (+ the X) reply X W   + of the replies K :   he summoned] having summoned M V :   his brothers and sons X :   his 1°] om S W :   his 2°]   om Z X K

    2 my sons and my brothers] M V   my brothers and sons K S   my brothers and my sons W   om rel :   by Israel] + of your father X :   my 3°---father]   to my words X : my 3°]   om K W :   my sons]   om S

    3 death] + and I was not envious K

    4 inc] Z W   + and rel :   of mine]   om L :   me 1° ---me 2°]   om X L :   they 1°]   and they X :   and 2°] but S :   my]   our Z W :   preserved]   saved K

    5 and 1°---captivity]   om W S* :   Lord 1°---Lord 2°] om K :   I was led into captivity]   om S :   I was led] I was sold M :   and his mighty---hunger]   om X L : mighty hand]   father's hand S W :   same] Z   *after* Lord M   om rel

    6 God]   + of my father X :   I was 2°]   om Z S W he is L :   and 2°]   om S W :   the Most High 1°]   God M L K S W   the solicitous one X   + aided me and K :

բանդի եւ բարձրեալն շնորհալից արար զիս. ի կապանս եւ արձակեաց զիս. 7 ի չարախաւսութիւնս՝ եւ քատագովեաց վասն իմ. ի բանդս դառինս եզիպտացւոց՝ եւ փրկեաց զիս. ի նախանձ ծառայակցաց՝ եւ բարձրացոյց զիս:

2:1 Եւ այսպէս Փոտիփար հաւատաց ինձ զտուն իւր: 2 Եւ հանդիսացայ ընդդէմ կնոջն անամաւթի, որ փութացուցանէր զիս մեղանչել ընդ ինքեան, այլ Աստուած իսրայելի հալր իմոյ փրկեաց զիս յայրմանէ հրոյն: 3 Բանդարգել եդէ, շարշարեցայ, արհամարհեցայ, եւ ետ զիս Տէր ի գթութիւնս առաջի բանդապետին: 4 Վասն զի ոչ թողու Տէր գերկիղոսս իւր, եւ ոչ խաւարեցուցանէ կապնաւք եւ կամ նեղութեամբք եւ կամ վտանկիւք. 5 Վասն զի ոչ եթէ իբրեւ զմարդ պատկառէ Աստուած, եւ ոչ իբրեւ զորդի մարդոյ վատասրտէ, եւ ոչ իբրեւ գերկրածին տկարանայ, եւ կամ մերժի. 6 Զի է յամենայն

խնամական X + աւգնեաց ինձ եւ K : ի բանդի եւ բարձրեալն] om K S W : բանդի] + եի M L + եդայ ես X : բարձրեալն 2°] աստուած M X L + այցելու եդեւ ինձ M + իմ X : կապանս] + եի X L K : եւ 4°] + տէր X + աստուած L : զիս 3°] որ W

7. չարախաւսութիւնս] չարութիւնս Z + էր W : եւ 1°] om L : բանդս] բանդի եի K : դառինս] om K S W : եզիպտացւոց] -ւոյն K : եւ 2°] + անդի X : զիս 1°---զիս 2°] om X L

2:1 փոտիփար] պետափրեւս K S W : ինձ] + ետ ինձ M :

2 իսրայելի] om X L post իմոյ K S W : հալր իմոյ] հարցն իմոց Z

3 եդէ] Z + եւ rel : արհամարհեցայ] Z om rel : գթութիւն Z M

4 տէր] post իւր Z om M L : նեղութեամբ X L K S W : վտանգիւ K

5 մարդ; K S W : որդի K S W : երկրածին K S W

1:6-2:6   TESTAMENT OF JOSEPH   17

the Most High made me graceful, in bonds and he loosed me,
7 Amidst calumnies and he defended me, in the bitter Egyptian
prisons and he delivered me, amidst the envy of my fellow-
slaves and he exalted me.

    2:1 And thus Potiphar entrusted his house to me. 2 And
I entered a contest with the shameless woman who urged me to
sin with her, but the God of Israel, my father, delivered me
from the burning of the fire. 3 I was imprisoned, I was tortured, I was despised, and the Lord made me the subject of the
warder's compassion. 4 Because the Lord does not abandon
those who fear him nor does he put them in darkness in bonds,
nor by tribulations, nor by misfortunes. 5 Because God is
not put to shame like a man, nor does he fear like a son of man,
nor is he powerless like the earth-born, nor is he driven out.
6 For he is in all places and he is besought in divers forms,

---

in prison---High 2°]   om   K S W :   prison]   + I was   M L
+ I was placed   X :   the Most High 2°]   God   M X L   + was
my visitor   M   + my   X :   bonds]   + I was   X L K :
he]   the Lord   X   God   L :   me 3°]   who   W

    7 inc]   + he was   W :   calumnies]   evils   Z :
and 1°]   om   L :   bitter]   om K S W :   prisons]   prison
K   + I was   K :   of the Egyptian   K :   and 2°]
+ thence   X :   me 2°---me 3°]   om   X L

    2:1 Potiphar]   Petap'rēs   K S W :   entrusted]   + he
gave   M

    2 of Israel]   om   X L   of my father Israel   K S W :
my father]   my fathers   Z

    3   imprisoned]   Z   + and rel :   I was despised]   Z
om   rel

    4   the Lord]   om   M L :   by tribulation X L K S W :
by misfortune   K

տեղիս, եւ ազգի ազգի ձեւաւք առաչի, դոյզն մի հեռացեալ առ ի փորձել զնոգլույն զխորհուրդն: 7 ի տասն փորձութիւնսն ընտիր զիս երեւեցոյց, եւ յամենայնս յայսոսիկ երկայնամիտ գտայ, զի մեծ դեղք են երկայնմտութիւն եւ բազում բարիս շնորհէ համբերութիւն:

3:1 Քանի՜զս անգամ եգիպտոցին սպանացաւ ինձ մահ, քանի՜զս անգամ տանչանաց մատնեալ, վերստին կոչեաց զիս եւ սպանացաւ ինձ, ոչ կամեցեալ իմ կամակատար նմա լինել: Եւ ասէր ինձ. 2 Տիրիցես ինձ եւ իմոցս ամենայնի, եթէ տացես զքեզ ինձ եղիցիս իբրեւ զտէրն իմ: 3 Բայց ես յիշեի զքանս հարց հալըն իմոյ Յակոբայ, եւ մտանեի ի սենեակն ալաւթս առնեի առ Տէր. 4 Եւ պահէի զեւթն զամսն զայնոսիկ, եւ երեւեի եգիպտացւոյն որպէս թէ փափկութեամբ վարեի:

6 է] post տեղիս KSW : յամենայն տեղիս] յամենայնի տէր X ամենայնի տէր L : առաչեի SW : եւ ոչ դոյզն (դոզն K) KSW : զնոգլոցն խորհուրդա Z

7 ի] post տասն M : յամենայն K յամենայնի S յամենայնէ W : յայսցիկ L : երկայնամիտ] ZM ընտիր rel : դեղք են] երկեղ է K գեղ է S : երկայնմտութիւն] -ութիւն ք MXL + համբերութիւնն KS + համբերութիւնք W : բազում] om XL : համբերողացն XLKS

3:1 եգիպտացին MXLKSW : տանչանաց] տանչեցայ X : մատնեաց L + եւ դարձեալ X + զիս S° W : զիս] om W : ինձ 2°] om KSW + այլ ես XL + եւ K : իմ] իսկ M : նմա լինել] Z լինել նմա rel

2 իմոցս] իմում MKS ի միում ամի W : տացես--- եղիցիս] տիրես ինձ համբիրեցեմ K : տացես] տիրիցես WS : ինձ զքեզ WS : եղիցիս] արարից ինձ S

3 զքան K : հարց] ZM*L eras Mc om rel : մտանեի] + առանձինն X : սենեակն] + եւ XLKW : առնելով Z : տէր] ասարած XL

4 պահէ] K : զամսն] զալուրսն MSW ալուրսն X ալր L ալուրս K : զայսոսիկ K : եւ 2°---վարեի] om KW : եգիպտոցյն MXL : որպէս] om XLS : փափկացեալ

2:6-3:4　　　　　　　TESTAMENT OF JOSEPH　　　　　　　　　　19

being a little distance away in order to test the thought of the soul. 7 In ten tests he showed me to be choice and in all these I was found to be longsuffering, for longsuffering is a great talisman and patience grants many good things.

3:1 How many times did the Egyptian woman threaten me with death? How many times, having delivered (me) to tortures, did she summon me anew and threaten me who did not desire to do her will? 2 And she said to me, 'You will possess me and all my goods if you give yourself to me; you will be like my master.' 3 But I remembered the words of the fathers of my father Jacob and I entered into (my) chamber, I prayed to the Lord. 4 And I fasted for those seven years and I appeared to the Egyptian as if I was living with pleasures,

---

　　　6 he is] *after* 'places' K S W :　　in all places]
Lord in everything　X　　Lord of everything　L :　　I was be-
seeching　S W :　　forms]　　+ and not　K S W :　　the thoughts
of the souls　Z

　　　7 in all]　　to each　K　　in each　S　　by each one　W :
longsuffering 1°]　Z M　　choice　rel :　　longsuffering 2°]
longsuffering (plur.)　M X L　　+ patience　K S　　+ patience
(plur.)　W :　　talisman]　fear　K　　beauty　S :　　patience]
to the patient ones　X L K S :　　many]　om　X L

　　　3:1 having delivered]　she delivered　L　　+ and again　X
+ me　S° W :　　to tortures]　I was tortured　X :　　me 3°]
om　W :　　me 4°]　om K S W　　+ but I　X L　　+ and　K

　　　2 all my goods]　in one year everything　W :　　you give]
you will possess　W S :　　to me yourself　W S :　　you will be]
I will make for me　S

　　　3 word　K :　　of the fathers]　Z M* L　　eras M^c　　om
rel :　　I entered]　+ on my own　X :　　chamber]　+ and　X L
K W :　　praying　Z :　　the Lord]　God　X L

　　　4 he fasts　K :　　these　K :　　years]　Z　　days　rel :
and---pleasures]　om　K W :　　Egyptian (masc. or fem.)]　Z
Egyptian woman　rel :　　as if]　om　X L S :　　I was living]
they were living　M　　I was　X L S :　　with pleasures]　Z
having engaged in pleasures　rel

զի որք վասն Աստուծոյ պահեն զհիմացն շնորհս առնուն։ 5 Եւ եթէ երթայի ուրեք, զինի ոչ ըմպեի, եւ գերիզ ալուրց զղարմանն առնուի եւ զայն տայի աղքատաց եւ հիւանդազ։ 6 Եւ առաւելտ առնեի առ Տէր, եւ լայի վասն Մեմփեա Եգիպտացւոյ վասն զի յոյժ եւ անպակաս շտապէր զիս, եւ ի գիշերի մտանէր առ իս պառնանաւէպ տեսանելոյ։ 7 Եւ վասն զի որդի առու ոչ էր նորա, պատճառէր առնել զիս ինքեան որդի։ Եւ աղաւթս արարի առ Տէր եւ ծնաւ որդի։ 8 Եւ ի բազում ժամանակս իբրեւ զորդւով գիրկս արկանէր զինեւ, եւ ես ոչ գիտէի։ Եւ յետ այսորիկ ի պոռնկութիւն կամեցաւ ձգել զիս։ 9 Եւ իմ իմացեալ, տրտմեցայ մինչեւ ի մահ։ Եւ եղեւ իբրեւ ել նա, եկին միտք իմ յիս,

---

M X L S : վարեի] վարին M : լինեի X L S

5 եւ 2°] om X L : ալուրցն M առեալ զղարմանն M X L S առեալ զղարմանս K առնեի զղարմանն W : եւ տայի--- հիւանդաց] om L : եւ 3°] om K S : զայն տայի] M S W տայի զայն X : զայն] om Z K : հիւանդացայ Z

6 inc] + այլ K S W : եւ 1°] + զգիշերն ամենայն աղաւթեի եւ W : տէր] աստուած L : մեմփեա M մեփայի X մեմփայի L մեմբթայ K S մեմթայ W : եգիպտացւոյն] Z + տինկոնչն իմ W : զիս] + առ ի գործել պոռնկութիւն W : եւ 3°] om K

7 արու որդի K : էր] գոյր K S W + ընդ M : էր նորա] ունէր նա X L : նորա] նմա K : զիս առնել M : զիս որդի առնել (առնւանել K) ինքեան K S W : որդի ինքեան M X L : տէր] + վասն նորա X

8 ի] om L : իբրեւ զորդւով] post զինեւ L : զորդւովք M : կամեցաւ ձգել] կոչեաց Z կամեցաւ արկանել (արկան K) K S W

9 եւ 1°] + ապա X : իմ] om K S : իմացեալ] զիտացեալ X : նա] + եւ K S : յիս] + եւ X L : սզացայ] + եւ լացի W : ալուրս M X L K S W : զի] om M K S W իբրեւ X

for those who fast for God's sake take on grace of countenance.
5 And if I went anywhere, I would drink no wine and I would
take the three-days' provisions and give them to the poor and
the sick. 6 And I would awake early for the Lord and weep on
account of Memp'ē the Egyptian, because she urged me strongly
and unceasingly, and at night she would enter my room on the
pretext of inspecting (me). 7 And because she had no male
child, she claimed to make me her son. And I prayed to the
Lord and she bore a son. 8 And for a long time she embraced
me like a son and I knew not (sc. her desire). And after this
she wished to drag me along into fornication. 9 And, having
understood (this), I was distressed unto death. And it was,
when she had

---

    5 and 2°]   om   X L :   I would take]   having taken
M X L S K   I would make W :   give---sick]   om L :
them]   om Z K :   the sick]   I was sick Z

    6 inc]   + but K S W :   and 1°]   + all the night I
would pray and W :   the Lord]   God L :   Memp'ē]   Z
various spelling variants   rel :   Egyptian (masc. or fem.)]
Z   Egyptian woman rel   + my mistress W :   me 1°] + to
commit fornication W :   and 3°]   om K :   my room] *lit.*
to me

    7 she had (*lit.* there was to her)]   she had X L :
to make]   to name K :   the Lord]   + for her sake X

    8 for]   om L :   a son]   sons M :   she wished to
drag...along]   she summoned Z   she wished to cast K S W

    9 and 1°]   + then X :   understood]   learned X :
out]   + and K S :   to me]   + and X L :   I sorrowed]
+ and I wept W :   for]   om M K S W   when X

սզացայ վասն նորա զաւուրս բազումս, զի զիտացի զնենգութիւն նորա եւ զմոլորութիւն։ 10 Եւ ասեի ցնա զբանս Բարձրելոյն, զի թերեւս դարձցի ի չար ցանկութենէ իւրմէ։

4:1 Քանի՞ցս անգամ իբրեւ սուրբ ատ բանիւք շողոքորթէր զիս, եւ նենգութեամբ բանից գովէր զպարկեշտութիւն իմ առաջի առն իւրոյ, կամեցեալ գայթակղեցուցանել զիս առանձին. 2 Փառաւորէր զիս յայտնապէս իբրեւ զպարկեշտ, եւ ի ծածուկ ասէր ցիս. Մի երկնչիր յառնէ իմմէ, վասն զի վստահացեալ է ի պարկեշտութիւնդ քո, զի թեպէտ ասիցէ ոք ցնա վասն մեր, ոչ հաւատայ։ 3 Յաղագս այսր ամենայնի գետնախշտի լինեի, եւ խորդովք պաղատեի Աստուծոյ, զի ապրեցուսցէ զիս յեղպատունէ։ 4 Եւ իբրեւ ոչ ինչ հանդուրժեաց, բանիւ վարդապետութեան մտանէր առ իս, կամելով ուսանել զբանս Տեառն։ 5 Եւ ասէր ցիս. Եթէ կամիս եթէ թողից զկուռսն, ընչեա առ իս. եւ

4:1 inc] + եւ ասէր S + եւ նա յայտնապէս առ աչս մարդկան ասէր W ։ քանիցս] om W ։ ցանգամ W ։ իբրեւ սուրբ առ] առ սուրբ K S W ։ առ] om X L ։ բանիւք] + քո K S W ։ եւ] om X ։ բանից] բանիւ X -իւք L K S W + որսայր զիս եւ K ։ գովէր] Z K + զիս rel +եւ X L S W ։ իմ] om X L ։ առաջի] om K ։ իւրոյ] + պատմէր զիմ եւ X + եւ ի ծածուկ W ։ կամեցաւ X K

2 inc] + եւ յայտնի X ։ յայտնապէս] om XL ։ ի] om Z S ։ է] om Z ։ զի 2°] եւ S ։ ցնա] om K ։ մեր] + ինչ W

3 յաղագս] եւ ես վասն X ։ խորդով L K S W ։ աստուծոյ] Z առ տէր rel

4 ինչ] Z om rel ։ բանիւ] Z բանին rel ։ իս] + եւ L ։ կամէր W

5 ցիս] Z W om rel: կամիմ] կամիմ Z կամիցիմ K ։ եթէ 2°] om K W ։ ընչել K ։ իս] + եւ կամ դեր ինձ W ։ զեզիպտացին] om X L -ոչիսն K + զայր իմ W ։ հաւանեցուցանեմ] + ես զայրն իմ X + զայրն իմ L ։ տեառն] om W

gone out, my sense came back to me. I sorrowed because of her for many days, for I learned her deceit and error. 10 And I said the words of the Most High to her so that, perhaps, she would turn aside from her evil desire.

4:1 How many times, as a saint, did she wheedle me with words and with guile of speech she lauded my modesty before her husband, desiring to scandalize me alone. 2 She praised me openly as modest and in secret she said to me, 'Do not fear my husband for he is confident of your modesty; for even if someone were to tell him about us, he would not believe (it).' 3 Because of all this I lay prostrate upon the ground and in sack-cloth I implored God to deliver me from the Egyptian woman. 4 And when she in no way held out against (sc. her desire), she entered to me by means of the discourse of instruction, by desiring to learn the Lord's words. 5 And she said to me, 'If you wish me to leave the idols, sleep with me and I will persuade the Egyptian to abandon the idols

---

4:1 inc] + and she would say S + and she openly before the eyes of men would say W : how many] om W : as a saint with] with your holy K S W : and] om X : of speech] with speech X L K S W : + she tried to seduce me and K : lauded] Z K + me rel + and X L S W : my] om X L : before] om K : husband] + she related mine, and X + and in secret W : she desired X K

2 inc] + and openly X : openly] om X L : in] om Z S : is] om Z : for] and S : him] om K + anything W

3 because] and I because X : God] Z the Lord rel

4 in no way] Z not rel : me] + and L : by means of discourse] Z (against) the discourse rel : by desiring] she desired W

5 to me] Z W om rel : I wish Z I will wish K : idols 1°] lacuna X : to sleep K : me] + or place for me W : the Egyptian] om X L the Egyptian women K + my husband W : I will persuade] + my husband X L :

գեզիպտացին հաւանեցուցանեմ ի բաց կալ ի կոցն, եւ յաւրինս Տեառն քո գնալ: 6 Եւ ասեմ գնա. Ոչ պղծութեամբ կամի Տէր զպաշտաւնեայս իւր, եւ ոչ հաճի ընդ շունս: 7 Եւ նա լուր եղեւ կարաւտելով կատարել զգանկութիւն իւր: 8 Եւ ես յաւելուլի ի պահս եւ յաղաւթս զի ապրեցուսցէ զիս Տէր ի նմանէ:

5:1 Խարձեալ յայլում ժամանակի ասէր զիս. Եթե շնացող ոչ կամիս լինել, ես սպանանեմ զեգիպտացին, եւ այսպէս ալրինաւք առնում զքեզ ինձ այր: 2 Իսկ ես իբրեւ լուայ զայս պատառեցի զպատմուճանն իմ եւ ասացի. Կին, դու պատկառ ի Տեառնէ, եւ մի առներ զայդ չար գործ, զի մի սատակեսցիս, վասն զի եւ ես պատմեցից զխորհուրդ ամբարշտութեանդ քո ամենեցունց: 3 Եւ երկուցեալ նորա աղաչէր զիս զի մի ումէք պատմեցից զչարութիւն նորա: 4 Եւ նորա գնացեալ ընծայիւք ջեռուցանէր զիս, եւ առաքէր ինձ զամենայն

---

6 գնա] om Z K: պղծութեամբ] post տէր X L K: իւր] + ծառայել նմա X: հաճի] Z + տէր rel: շունս] + եւ ընդ պոոնիկս W

7 լուր] + լինէր Z: եղեւ] + եւ L S: կարաւտելով կատարել] կատարելով K S W: զգանկութիւն] Z զկամն M զկամս rel: իւր] իմ K S W

8 յաւելուլի] post յաղաւթս Z: յաղաւթս եւ ի պահս L K S W

5:1 յայլ W: ասէր] + կին W: կամիս լինել] լինիս K S W: զեգիպտացին] + զայրն իմ W: եւ] + ապա Z: այսպէս] om K S

2 իսկ] եւ X: զայս] om K S W: զայդ չար] զչար K S W: գործ ծ M S զգործծ ante զայդ X L գործուղ W: եւ 3°] om K: պատմիցեմ W: զխորհուրդ ամբարշտ.] զչար գործ ծ M L զչար գործ ծս X S W զգործ ծս K

3 երկուցեալ նորա] om K S նա W: պատմեցից] ասացից M K W ասիցեմ X L: զչարին M զչարիս X L K S W

4 եւ նորա] om K: վայելչութիւն L

and to walk in the law of your Lord.' 6 And I said to her, 'Not through abomination does the Lord desire those who minister to him nor is he pleased with adulterers.' 7 And she was silent, wishing to fulfil her desire. 8 And I continued to fast and pray that the Lord might deliver me from her.

5:1 Again, at another time, she said to me, 'If you do not wish to be an adulterer, I (will) kill the Egyptian and thus I (will) legally take you as my husband.' 2 But I, when I heard this, rent my garment and said, 'Woman, have shame before the Lord and do not do this evil deed lest you be killed, because even I will proclaim your plan of impiousness to all.' 3 And being afraid, she beseeched me not to proclaim her wickedness to anybody. 4 And she, departing, warmed me with gifts and sent me all delights of the sons of men.

Lord]   om   W

    6 to her]   om   Z K :   through abomination]   *after* desire   X L K :   to him]   + to serve him   X :   he]   Z   the Lord   rel :   adulterers]   + and with harlots   W

    7 was]   + also   L S :   wishing to fulfil]   fulfilling K S W :   her]   my   K S W :   desire]   Z   will   rel

    8 I continued]   *after* pray   Z :   to pray and fast   L K S W

    5:1 she]   the woman   W :   you do not wish to be]   you are not   K S W :   the Egyptian]   + my husband   W :   and] + then   Z :   thus]   om   K S

    2 but]   and   X :   this 1°]   om   K S W :   this evil] the evil   K S W :   deed]   *before* evil   X L   deeds   W : even]   om   K :   plan of impiousness]   evil deed   M L evil deeds   X S W   deeds   K

    3 being afraid]   om   K S W :   proclaim]   Z S   tell rel :   wickedness]   Z   evils   rel

    4 and she]   om   K :   delight   L

ԿՏԱԿ ՅՈՎՍԵՓԱՅ

վայելչութիւնս որդւոց մարդկան:

6:1 Առաքեաց ինձ եւ կերակուր կախարդութեամբ թաթաւեալ: 2 Եւ իբրեւ եկն ներքինին որ բերէր ինձ գդարմանն, ի վեր հայեցեալ եւ տեսի այր ահաւոր որ տայր ցիս հանդերձ պատենիւք սուր, եւ գիտացի եթէ նենգութիւնս այս ի մոլորութիւն է ինձ: 4 Եւ եղեւ իբրեւ ել նա արտաքս սկսայ լալ եւ ոչ զայն եւ ոչ յայլոց խորտկաց նորա ճաշակեցի։ 4 Եւ յետ միոյ աւուր եկեալ նորա առ իս, ծանեաւ զկերակուրն եւ ասէ ցիս. Զի՞նչ է այս զի ոչ կերար ի կերակրոյս: 5 Եւ ասեմ ցնա. Վասն զի լցեր զդրոսա մահուամբ. եւ զիա՞րդ ասացեր եթէ ոչ մերձենամ ի կոյս, այլ միայն առ Տէր: 6 Արդ այժմ ծանիր զի Աստուած հալըն իմոյ ի ձեռն տրեշտակին իւրոյ յայտնեաց ինձ զչարութիւնդ քո, եւ պահեցի զայդ յանդիմանութիւն քեզ զի թերեւս տեսեալ ապաշխարեսցես:

6:1 եւ] Z   om rel   :   կերակուրս X

 2 եւ 1°] om K + եղեւ Z: գդարմանն] զկերակուրն W : եւ 2°] Z om rel: այր] + մի X : ահաւոր K S* W : որ] զի X եւ L : հանդերձս K S : սուր] սուրբ K S ante հանդ. W : գիտացի] K S W ագացի rel : նենգ.--- մոլոր.] մոլորութիւնն այն ի նենգաւորութիւն X մոլորութիւնս այս ի նենգութիւն L : այս] om K S : մոլորութիւն է] մոլորութենէ S W

 3 եւ---արտաքս] Z om rel : եւ սկսայ X L S° սկաւ K S* W : լալ] om K S* W ; զայն---յայլոց] զայլ ինչ ի K : յայլ M X L S W + ի M : խորտրդակաց L

 4 միւսոյ X L միւս այլ W իմոյ K : նորա] om K : ծանեաւ զկերակուրն] om K S W : զկերակուրն] M L զկերակուրն rel : կերակրոյս] M K կերակրոցս rel + յայս S W

 5 վասն] om X L : կուռօն M: միայն] Z om rel

 6 արդ] Z եւ rel : զի աստուած] զաստուած K S* W : հարցն իմոց M X L K S W + եւ K + զի W : ինձ] X K S B om rel : եւ 2°] մի K S* W + ես X : պահեցի K S -եցէ W :: քո K S W : տեսցես եւ M X L K S W

6:1 She also sent me food drenched with magic charms.
2 And when the eunuch who was bringing me the provisions came, I looked up and saw a fearsome man who was giving me a sword with a scabbard. And I knew that this deception was (designed) to lead me astray. 3 And it was, when he went outside, I began to cry and I did not eat that nor any of her other dishes.
4 And after one day, having come to me she recognized the food and said to me, 'Why is it that you did not eat of this food?'
5 And I said to her, 'Because you filled them with death; and how did you say, "I will not approach idols, but only the Lord"?
6 Now, therefore, know that the God of my father revealed your wickedness to me through his angel and I kept it as a reproach for you so that, perhaps having seen (it) you might repent.

6:1   also] Z   om rel :   sent] dispatched K W : foods X

2   and 1°]   om K   + it was Z :   provisions] food W :   and 2°]   Z   om rel :   a 1°]   + certain X : who]   that X   and L :   sword]   holy K S :   knew] K S W   sorrowed rel :   this deception was (designed) to lead...astray]   that (this L) leading astray was for deception X L :   this]   om K S :   to lead me astray]   lit. for an error for me

3 and---outside] Z   om rel :   and I began X L S° he (or: she) began K S* W :   to cry] om K S* W :   that ---other]   anything else of K :   of another of her dishes M X L S W

4 one]   another X L   other other W   my K : recognized the food]   om K S W :   food 1°] M L   foods rel :   food 2°] M K   foods rel

5 because]   for X L :   the idol M :   only] Z om rel

6 therefore] Z   and rel :   that the God]   the God K S* W :   father] Z   fathers rel   + and K   + that W :   to me] X K S B   om rel :   and I kept it]   let it not be kept K S*   let him not keep W :   having seen] you might see (it) and M X L K S W

7 եւ զայս գիտասջիր, զի որք պարկեշտութեամբ զնստուած պաշտեն, ոչ հանդարտէ շարութիւն ամբարշտաց։ Եւ առեալ առաջի նորա կերայ ի խորտկէն եւ ասացի. Աստուած հարց իմոց եւ հրեշտակն Աբրահամու եղիցի ընդ իս։ 8 Եւ նա անկեալ ի վերայ երեսաց իւրոց յոտս իմ ելաց. եւ իմ յարուցեալ զնա խրատեի։ 9 Եւ ուխտեաց ընդ իս ոչ եւս գործել զամբարշտութիւնս զայս։

7:1 Սակայն եւ եւս էր սիրտ նորա շոյլեալ ընդ իս եւ յոզւոց հանելով տրտմէր. 2 Եւ տեսեալ զնա եգիպտացւոյն սաէր զնա. Ընդէ՞ր ի վայր են անկեալ երեսք քո։ Եւ նա ասէ. Ցաւ սրտի իմ ցաւէ եւ հնչմունք սրտիս իմոյ արգելուն զիս. եւ ողջացուցանէր զնա զոչ հիւանդացեալն։ 3 Ցայնժամ վազեալ նորա առ իս մինչդեռ

---

7 աստուածապաշտին M L K S : ոչ հնարն lacuna պատրէ եւ W : խորտկացն X : ասացի] + զնա X L : աբրահամու---իս] Z նորա պահեցէ զիս rel

8 անկեալ] + առաջի իմ K : յոտս իմ] om X L : յարուցեալ] մատուցեալ X L : խրատեի զնա X : խոտեցի K

9 ընդ իս] ինձ X L cf.6:6 : եւս] om K S : գործել] + ընդ իմ K : զամբարշտութիւնսն M -ութիւնն X զանաւրէնութիւնս K զանաւրէնութիւնն S W : զայն W

7:1 եւ եւս] Z om rel : էր] post նորա M X L

2 զնա] + առն իւրոյ X : զնա] Z om rel : են] կան K S W : են անկեալ] Z անկեալ են rel : երեսք M : նա] կինն W : ցաւ] om K S W : սիրտ K : ինձ] իմոյ X L S W իմ K : հնչումն K : սրտիս] Z սրտի M L K S W երդի X : արգելոյ K -ելու S : ողջ. զնա] Z նա ողջ. rel: զի մի հիւանդանայցէ K S W

3 inc] + եւ ընդ անցանելն (յանց. K) իմ K S W : յայնժամ] եւ յալուրն երկրորդի X : խեղդեմ M : զիս 1°---զիս 2°] om K S W : ընկենում զիս 2°] om X L անկանիմKSW

7 And know this, that the wickedness of the impious does not withstand those who serve God with modesty.' And taking hold (of it) I ate some of the food in front of her and I said, 'May the God of my fathers and the angel of Abraham be with me!' 8 And she, having fallen on her face at my feet, wept. And I, having raised her up, admonished (her). 9 And she undertook to me to do this impiety no more.

7:1 However, her heart still also lusted after me and, sighing, she was sad. 2 And the Egyptian, having seen her, said to her, 'Why has your face fallen?' And she said, 'A pain of the heart distresses me and the sounds of my heart constrict me.' And he cured her who was not ill. 3 Then she ran to me while her

---

7 that] + intrigue (lacuna) does not overcome and W : foods X : said] + to her X L : the angel of Abraham be with] Z his angel protect rel

8 having fallen] + before me K : at my feet] om X L : having raised her up] having brought her near X L : admonished] scorned K

9 to do] + with me K : this] that W : impiety] lawlessness K S W : no more] not K S.

7:1 still also] Z om rel

2 the Egyptian] her husband the Egyptian X : to her] Z om rel : she] the woman Z : pain om K S W : of the heart...me] my heart K of my heart X L S W : sound K : heart 2°] liver X : constricts K S : her] Z he rel : who---ill] that she might not be ill K S W

3 inc] + and at my passing by K S W : then] and on the second day X :

էր այր նորա արտաքոյ եւ ասէր ցիս. Կամ խեղդիմ կամ ի ջրհոր ընկենում զիս եւ կամ ի վախից ի վայր ընկենում զիս եթէ ոչ ննջեսցես ընդ իս: 4 Եւ իմ իմացեալ եթէ հոգի բելիարայ զնա շտապէ, աղաւթս արարեալ առ Տէր ասացի զնա. 5 Ընդէ՞ր խռովիս եւ կամ ամբոխիս ի մեղս կուրացեալդ. յիշեա զայս, զի եթէ սպանանիցես զքեզ, Ասիթոյ հարճ առն քո հակառակորդ քո կովահարեսցէ զորդին քո եւ կորուսցէ զյիշատակ քո յերկրէ: 6 Եւ ասէ ցիս. Ատաղադիկ սիրեցեր զիս. բաւական է ինձ այս, զի հոգաս վասն կենաց իմոց եւ վասն որդւոց իմոց. արդ ակն ունիմ վայելել ի ցանկութեանս իմում: 7 Եւ ոչ իմացաւ եթէ վասն Աստուծոյ իմոյ ասացի այսպէս եւ ոչ վասն նորա: 8 Զի եթէ յախտս այսպիսիս յանցգնութեանց եւ շարեաց ոք անկանիցի, որպէս եւ նա, եւ նմա ծառայիցէ, թէպէտ եւ քարի ինչ

---

    4 իմացեալ] զիտացեալ X : հոգին M L ոգին X : զնա շտապէ] Z շտապէ զնա rel : շտապեցուցանէ K S W : արարի X L K S W : տէր] + եւ X L K S : զնա] զկինն W
    5 ամբոխիս (+ եւ S) կամ խռովիս K S W : եւ 1°] om L K : մեղս] տեղիս յայս W : կուրացեալդ] Z կարեւորս կոռուսեալդ rel + յոյժ K S W : յիշեա] զիտեա K S զիտասցիր W : զայդ X L : զի] Z om rel : եթէ] էր K : ասիթոյ] ասեի թէ (եթէ W) K S W : հարճ] հանձար K S : հարճ առն քո] խորհուրդն քո W : հակառակորդ քո] K S* W հառառակ որդյն քո M հակ. որդւոյ քո X L S° om Z : քո 2°---քո 3°] om K : կովահարեսցէ] կովեսցէ M կովիցէ X կովիցէ L կովէ զքեզ S W : զորդին M L որդին W
    6 ցիս] +կինն W : ատաղասիկ M X L om K S W: զիս---զի] om K S* W + եւ W : այս զի] om S° : կենաց] մահուան K S W : իմոց 1°---իմոց 2°] om X L K S W: իմոց 1°] իմոյ K S W : ցանկութիւնս X L K S W
    7 այսպէս] M X L զայս rel
    8 յախտոյ X L : յայսպիսիս M K S W այսպիսի X L : յանցգնեցի K : եւ 3°] om X L S W: նմա] om W: քարի]

husband was outside and said to me, 'I will choke myself or I will cast myself into a well or I will cast myself down from precipices if you will not sleep with me.' 4 And I, understanding that a spirit of Beliar was urging her on, having prayed to the Lord I said to her, 5 'Why are you disturbed or upset, having been blinded in sins? Remember this, that if you kill yourself, Asit'o your husband's concubine, your rival, will smite your children and destroy your memory from the earth.' 6 And she said to me, 'Behold! You love me. This is sufficient for me, that you care about my life and about my children. Now I have hope of finding pleasure in this desire of mine.' 7 And she did not understand that I spoke thus because of my God and not because of her. 8 For if one falls into these sorts of rash and evil passions, as she did, and becomes enslaved to (them), even though he hear

---

I will choke M   + and M :   or 2°---precipices]   om K S W :   I will cast myself 2°]   om X L   I will fall K S W

    4 understanding]   knowing X :   the spirit M L X :   prayed X L K S W :   Lord]   + and X L K S :   to her]   to the woman W

    5 upset or disturbed K S W :   having been blinded in] Z   have perished in noteworthy rel   + exceedingly K S W :   sins]   this place W :   remember]   know K S W :   this]   that X L :   that] Z   om rel :   if]   he was K :   Asit'o]   I was saying that K S W :   your husband's concubine]   your plan W :   concubine]   genius K S :   your rival] K S* W   your son's rival M X L S°   om Z :   rival---children]   om K :   will smite]   will hammer L + you S W :   child (or: son) M X L W

    6 she]   the woman W :   behold]   om K S W :   me 1°---that]   om K S* W   + and W :   this ... that]   om S° :   life]   death K S W :   and about my children]   om X L K S W :   desires X L K S W

    7 thus] M X L   this rel

    8 falls]   is rash K :   rash---passions] *lit.* passions of rashness and evils: passion 1° X L :   and 2°]   om X L S W :   (them)] ed   om W   it rel:

լցէ, յախիցն յորոց յաղթեալ իցէ, զնոյն կարծէ վասն չար ցանկու-
թեանն իւրոյ։

8:1 Արդ ասեմ ձեզ, որդեակք իմ, զի ժամ էր իբրեւ վեցերորդ
յորժամ զնաց յինէն արտաքս, եւ իմ ծունր խոնարհեցուցեալ առ Տէր
զամենայն տիւ եւ զամենայն գիշեր միահամուռ, մաւտ յառաւաւտն յարեայ
արտասուելով առ Տէր եւ խնդրելով զփրկութիւն յեգիպտոցւոյն։ 2 Եւ
յետ այսորիկ բուռն եհար գճանդերձից իմոց, եւ բռնաբար ձզէր զիս զի
ննչեցից ընդ նմա։ 3 Եւ ես իբրեւ տեսի եթէ մոլեցուցեալ ըմբռնեաց
գճանդերձից իմոց, մերկացեալ փախեայ։ 4 Եւ ապա նորա զրպարտեալ

Z բիւր M X L   բնաւ K S W :   յախիցն] յաղթիցն S :
յորոց] Z   om rel :   կարծեալ M X K W -ել L S
+ լինի K :   վասն] Z   եւ առն M եւ առ   rel

8:1 յորժամ] եւ K S W :   իմ] ես W   post ծունր X :
խոնարհեցուցեալ] -ցուցի W   կրկնեալ X L :   զամենայն 2°]
om K S :   միահամուռ] + եւ X K S W :   մաւտ յառաւ.] ընդ
առաւ. L W :   յառուցեալ L K :   յարտասուելոյ (-ելոյն W)
K S W :   զփրկութիւն] + ինձ K S   praepon. ինձ W :   եգիպ-
տոցւոյն L   + մեմթայ W

2 այսորիկ] + եւ M   + եկեալ X :   եւ 2°] om K S
W :   բռնաբար] post զիս M L K S W :   ձզեալ բռնաբար X :
զիս] om X :   զի ննչեցից] Z   ննչել rel :   նմա] Z   իս
M   ինքեան rel

3 inc] + եւ ես թողի ի նա գճանդերձն եւ փախեայ արտաքս
W   sign for insertion after տայ նմա (vs. 4) W :   իբրեւ]
om M L K S W :   տեսեալ K S W :   մոլեզնեալ] + է X L :
ըմբռնեաց---fin] om K S W :   բռնեաց M   բռնեալ L   թողի
X :   փախեայ] + ի նմանէ X

4 եւ ապա նորա] տայ նմա K W   տայ նորա S   + եւ
նորա W :   զիս 1°---եզիպտացին] մատնեաց առն իւրում եւ եզիպտացին արկ զիս ի բանտ ի տան իւրում X :   զիս 1°] + առ այրն
իւր W B :   տանչեաց X L :   զիս 2°] + եւ X L W :
առաքեաց] + զիս K S

7:8-8:4   TESTAMENT OF JOSEPH   33

a good thing, he accounts it to the passions by which he has
been vanquished, because of his evil desire.

8:1 Now, I say to you, my children, that it was about the
sixth hour when she went outside from me and I, having bent my
knees to the Lord for the whole day and the whole night together, arose close to dawn weeping to the Lord and begging salvation from the Egyptian woman. 2 And after this she grasped
my garments and forcibly dragged me so that I might sleep with
her. 3 And when I saw that, crazed, she seized my garments
(or, *following* X Bb *cf.* W: she was crazed, I left my garment
and), having disrobed I fled. 4 And then, she having calum-
niated me,

---

good] Z   myriad M X L   totally K S W :   having ac-
counted M X K W   to account L S   + is K :   passions 2°]
victorious ones S :   by which] Z   om rel :   because of]
Z   and of the man M   and to rel

    8:1 when]   and   K S W :   having bent]   bent W
having doubled X L :   the whole 2°]   om K S :   and arose
X K S W :   having arisen L K :   at dawn L W :   to weep
K S W :   salvation]   + for me   K S W :   from]   om L :
woman]   + Memt'a W

    2 this]   + and   M   + having come X :   and 2°]   om
K S W :   forcibly]   *after* me M L K S W :   having dragged
forcibly X :   me]   om X :   so---sleep]   Z   to sleep
rel :   her]   me M

    3 inc]   + and I left to her (my) garment and fled out-
side W   *sign for insertion after*'she gives to him' (vs 4,
app.) W :   when]   Z X   om rel :   having seen K S W :
she was crazed X L :   seized---fin]   om K S W :   having
seized L   I left X :   my garment and X :   fled]
+ from her   X

    4 and then she]   she gives to him K W   she gives, she
S   + and she W :   me 1°---house]   she delivered (me) to
her husband and the Egyptian cast me into prison in his house
X :   me 1°]   + to her husband W B :

զիս, ի բանդ արկ ի տան իւրում եզիպտացին, եւ ի վադիւն տանջեալ
զիս ատաքեաց ի բանդն Փարաւոնի: 5 Եւ մինչդեռ ես ի կալանս էի,
եզիպտուհին հիանդանայր ի տրամութեանէն. եւ լսէր ինձ հանապազ որպէս աւրհնեի գտէր մինչ էի ի խաւարային տան, զուարթ ձայնիւ եւ
խնդալով փառաւորէի զԱստուած, զի միայն որոշեաց զիս ի պատճառանաց
եզիպտուհին։

9:1 Եւ բազում անգամ յղեաց առ իս եւ ասէ թե. Համեցաք ընդ իս
եւ արձակեմ զքեզ ի կապանացդ։ 4 Եւ թեպէտ ի հիանդութեան էր՝
իշաներ տարաժամու եւ լսէր ձայնի իմում որ աղաւթեի, եւ իմ իմացեալ
զհառաչանս նորա, լուռ լինէի: 5 Արդ մինչդեռ էի ես ի տան նորա,
մերկացուցանէր զթագուկս իւր եւ զկուրծս եւ զսրունս, զի զայթակ-
ղեցուցանէ զիս յինքն եւ զարդարէր զինքն յոյժ, բայց Տէր պահէր
զիս ի ձեռնարկութենէ նորա։

_____

5 եզիպտացին K : հիանդանայր եզիպտուհին X : ինձ]
om X L : որպէս աւրհնեի զտէր] om K : որպէս] + եւ M որ
ես X + զի L : խաւարին M խաւարի K S W : զուարթ
ձայնիւ] ante մինչ X : խնդալով] om X L խնդութեամբ K
S W : փառաւորէի] փառաւորելով աւրհնէի X L փառաւորել K:
զի] որ X

9:1 եւ 1°] Z զի rel : անգամ] om K S* W : եւ
ասէ] K S W om rel : իս 2°] իմ M + ի բանտն X + եւ
արա զկամս իմ K

4 թեպէտ եւ K S W : էր ի հիանդութ. M X L K S W :
տատաժամու] Z ի տարաժամ աւուրն rel + եւ յերեկորեանն ընդ
մութն W : զձայն X : իմում] իմ X իմոյ S W + եւ
յոգւոց հանէր X : որ աղաւթեի] W B om rel: իմացեալ]
զիտացեալ X : նորա] + եւ W

5 արդ] Z եւ X W om rel : մինչ K* : իւր] Z
K W om rel : զկուրծս] + եւ ի վեր ունելով զստորոտան K :
զսրունս M + իւր MC V + ոտիցն X : զի] ի K S :
զայթակղեցուցցէ M -ցուցանէր X -ցուցանէլ K S : յինքն]
Z om rel : եւ զարդարէր---յոյժ] om X L: զարդարէր

8:4-9:5   TESTAMENT OF JOSEPH   35

the Egyptian cast me into prison in his house. And on the next
day, having tortured me, he dispatched (me) to Pharaoh's prison.
5 And while I was in detention, the Egyptian woman fell ill
from sorrow, and she listened to me continually, how I blessed
the Lord while I was in the dark house: with a glad voice and
rejoicing I praised God for he had set me apart, alone from the
pretences of the Egyptian woman.

9:1 And many times she sent to me and said, 'Consent to
me and I will release you from (your) bonds.' 4 And although
she was ill she would descend at an unfitting time and listen
to my voice who was praying. And I, perceiving her sighs, was
silent. 5 Now, while I was in her house, she bared her arms
and breast and legs so that she might make me stumble to her,
and she adorned herself greatly, but the Lord preserved me from
her aggression.

---

he tortured X L :   me 2°]   + and X L W :   (me) 3°]   me
K S

    5 to me]   om   X L :   how---Lord]   om   K :   how]
+ and M who I X   + that L :   of the darkness M   of
darkness K S W :   with a glad voice]   *before* while X :
rejoicing]   om   X L   with joy K S W :   I praised]
praising I blessed   X L   to praise K :   for]   who X

    9:1   and 1°] Z   for rel :   times]   om K S* W :
and said]   K S W   om rel :   me 2°]   + in the prison   X
+ and do my will   K

    4 although also K S W :   at---time] Z   on an un-
fitting day rel   + and in the evening with dark   W :
voice]   + and would sigh X :   who was praying] W B   om
rel :   perceiving]   knowing   X

    5 now]   Z   and X W   om rel :   her 2°]   Z K W
om rel$_c$:   breast]   + and holding up her skirt K :   her
legs M^c V   + of feet X :   to make me stumble K S :
to her] Z   om rel :   and she---greatly]   om X L :
adorned herself]   having adorned M K S :   but]   and
M X L

10:1 Արդ տեսէք որդեակք իմ, որպիսի ինչ է հանդարտութիւն, եւ առաւէլ հանդերձ պահապք: 2 Եւ դուք, եթէ լինիցիք այնպիսիք, ի ցաւոց եւ ի չարէ եւ ի նեղութենէ փրկեսջիք ձեռամբ Տեառն, 4 Վասն զի կամ բանիւ եւ կամ խորհրդով յանցանիցէ ոք: 5 Արդ գիտեն եղբարք իմ թէ որպէս սիրեաց զիս հայրն իմ, եւ ոչ բարձրացուցի զանձն իմ թեպէտ եւ տղայ եի. զի գիտեի եթէ ամենայն ինչ անցանելոց է: 6 Եւ չափեի զանձն իմ եւ զնոսա պատուեի եւ վասն երկիւղի նոցա լուռ լինեի յորժամ վածտեին զիս, եւ ոչ ասեի ցիմայելացին վասն ազգին իմոյ, եթէ որդի եմ Յակոբայ, առն մեծի եւ զաւրաւորի:

11:1 Եւ դուք պատուեցէք զեղբարս ձեր, վասն զի ամենայն որ առնէ զաւրէնս Տեառն սիրեցի ի նմանէ: 2 Արդ եկեալ իմ ընդ նոսա ի Հնդկակոպացիսն, հարցանեին զիս համայելացիքն եւ ասեին ցիս,

զինքն] զարդարեալ M K S : բայց] եւ M X L այլ K S W
10:1 իմ] + թէ X W : ինչ] om K : էր X : հանդերձ] + ժուժկալութեամբ եւ X
2 այսպիսիք X K S : չարութենէ M : չարէ---նեղութ.] նեղութենէ...չարէ L K S W նեղութեանց եւ ի փորձութեանց եւ ի չարչարանաց X : փրկել ապրեսջիք X
4 վասն] Z om rel : զի] + եթէ W : կամ] om W : բանիւ] M K բանիւք rel : եւ] om X L K* S W : խորհր-դով] M X K W խորհրդովք rel : յանցանիցէ ոք] M K S W յանցանեմ Z ցանկանիցէք X յանցանիցէք L
5 արդ] Z om rel : գիտեմ S գիտէք W : զիս] om X : բարձրացուցանեի K S W : է] էր S W
6 համայելացւոցն X L om K S W: իմոյ] + եթէ յոր ազգէ եմ եւ ոչ W : Յակոբայ] om X L
11:1 եւ 1°] արդ L : դուք] + որդեակք իմ X : պատուեցէք] Z սիրեցէք rel : ձեր] + եւ Z : առնէ] սիրէ X K
2 Հիկկապոտացիսն K Հինգկիպապացիսն S Հինգկապոպացիսն W : զիս] ցիս W : ցիս] Z om rel : իս] om X K : բնութենէ L K S + է K : դոցա] + զայս ասացի X : զի]

10:1 Now you see, my children, of what character composure is, and prayer together with fasting. 2 And you, if you will be of that kind, will be saved by the Lord's hand from pains and from evil and from tribulation. 4 Because either by word or by thought a man might transgress. 5 Now, my brothers, know how my father loved me and I did not elevate myself, although I was a child, for I knew that everything is going to pass away. 6 And I moderated myself and I honoured them, and because of the fear of them I was silent when they were selling me and I did not say (anything) to the Ishmaelites concerning my family, that I was the son of Jacob, a great and powerful man.

11:1 And you, honour your brothers because everyone who does the Lord's law will be loved by him. 2 Now I, having come with them to the Indokopites, the Ishmaelites asked me and said to me,

---

    10:1   is]   was   X :   with]   + continence and   X

    2   of this kind   X K S :   evil]   wickedness   M :   evil and from tribulation]   tribulation and from evil   L K S W   tribulations and from trials and from tortures   X

    4   because]   Z   for rel :   either]   if   W :   word]   M K   words   rel :   thought]   M X K W   thoughts   rel :   a man might transgress]   M K S W   I transgress   Z   you might be in need   X   you might transgress   L

    5   now]   Z   om rel :   I know   S   you know   W :   me]   om   X :   I used...to elevate   K S W :   is]   was   S W

    6   Ishmaelites]   om   K S W :   family]   + or of which family I was, nor   W :   of Jacob]   om   X L

    11:1   and 1°]   now   L :   you]   + my children   X: honour]   Z   love rel :   brothers]   + and   Z :   does]   loves   X K

    2   Indokopites]   various variant spellings   K S W :   to me]   Z   om rel :

ԿՏԱԿ ՅՈՎՍԵՓԱՅ 11:2-12:1

ծառայ ես թե ազատ։ Եւ ես ասեի եթե. ծառայ եմ, ի բռնութենէ դղցա գի մի յամաւթ արարից գեղբարսն իմ։ 3 Եւ ասէ ցիս աւագն նոցա. Ոչ ես դու ծառայ, վասն գի եւ դէմք քո յայտնեն վասն քո։ Եւ նա սպառնայր ինձ բայց սակայն ես ասեի եթե ծառայ եմ։ 4 Արդ յորժամ եկաք յեգիպտոս վասն իմ կռուեին նորա, եւ իւրաքանչիւր ոք տայր գմասն վաճառոց իւրեանց, գի գիս ացեն ընդ շահից իւրեանց։ 5 Յաղագս որոյ ամենեցուն հածոյ թուեցաւ թողուլ գիս յեգիպտոսի առ փոխողի վաճառացն իւրեանց, մինչեւ դարձցին այսրէն եւ բերցեն գվաճառսն։ 6 Եւ Տէր ետ ինձ շնորհս առաջի աշաց փոխավաճառին եւ հաւատաց յիս գտուն իւր, 7 Եւ աւրհնեաց գնա Տէր ի ձեռս իմ, եւ բազմացոյց գարծաթ եւ գոսկի։ 8 Եւ եղէ առ նմա գամիսս երիս եւ գաւուրս հինգ։

12:1 Արդ անցեալ ընդ այն Մեմփիու կին Պետափրեայ եւ հայեցեալ

վասն գի W։ մի] om M

3 վասն 1°] om L։ եւ 2°] om K S։ վասն քո] գքեզ K S W։ ինձ] +եթէ գօշմարիտն ասա X

4 եկաք] om K S իշաք W։ վասն իմ] om K S W։ վաճառոյ K -ու S W։ իւրեանց 1°---իւրեանց 2°] om L։ իւրեանց 1°] +փոխան ինձ W։ գի] + եւ X։ ընդ---իւրեանց] om X։ շահու K S W

5 թուեցա M թուեցաւլ K S։ թողուլ] om K S։ յեգիպտոս M X L K S W + գրաւական W։ փոխ կողի K փոխկղի S։ անդրէն X L այսր W։ գվաճառն K + եւ արարին այսպէս W

6 աշաց] Z om rel։ փոխավաճ.] + իւրեանց K S W

7 ի ձեռս] յոտս X ձեռն L S։ գարծաթ եւ գոսկի] Z գոսկի եւ գարծաթ rel։ գարձայս X։ fin]+ նորա X + փոխավաճառիս W + իւր K

8 նա M։ գամիսս երիս] om X։ ամիս M^c ամիսս L K S W։ աւուրս M X L K S W։ հինգ] ու. X

12:1 անցանէր W։ մեմփիու]X L K S W մեմթենու Z

'Are you a slave or a free man?' And I said, 'I am a slave,' because of their violence, so that I should not put my brothers to shame. 3 And their chief said to me, 'You are not a slave, because your very face reveals (this) about you.' And he threatened me, but nonetheless I said, 'I am a slave.' 4 Now, when we came to Egypt, they quarrelled because of me, and each wanted to give part of his goods so that he might take me instead of his profits. 5 Because of this, it seemed pleasing to them all to leave me in Egypt with the dealer in their goods until they returned again and brought goods. 6 And the Lord gave me grace in the eyes of the dealer and he entrusted his house to me. 7 And the Lord blessed him through me and multiplied (his) silver and gold. 8 And I was with him for three months and five days.

12:1 Now, Memp'iu, wife of Petap'rē passed by there and, having

---

are you] om X K : violence] nature L K S + it is K + I said this X : so that] because W : not] om M

3 because] for L : very] om K S : about you] you K S W : me] + say the truth X

4 we came] om K S we went down W : because of me] om K S W : goods] + instead of me W : so that ---profits] om L : that] + also X : instead---profits] om X : profit K S W

5 I seemed M having seemed K S : to leave] om K S + a surety W : again] to this place W : goods 2°] good K + and they did thus W

6 in the eyes of] Z before rel : their dealer K S W

7 through (lit. at my hands)] at my feet X my hand L S : (his)] ed his X K the dealer's W : silver and gold] Z gold and silver rel : silver (plur.) X

8 for three---days] 95 days X

12:1 Memp'iu] X L K S W cf. 3:6, 14:5 Memt'iu Z Semp'iu M + who was W

տեսանէր զիս։ 2   Եւ ասէ ցայրն իւր վասն զվաշտափոխին, եթէ հար-
ստացաւ ի ծեռն մանկան ուրում երրայեցւոյն, եւ ասեն թէ գողու-
թեամբ գողացան զնա յերկրէն Քանանացւոց։ 3 Արդ, այժմ արա ընդ
նմա դատաստան եւ առ զմանուկն ի տնտեսութիւն քեզ, եւ աւրհնեսցէ
զքեզ Աստուածն երրայեցւոց զի շնորհք հաստատութեան են ի նմա։

13։1 Զուարթացեալ ընդ բանս նորա, հրամայեաց ածել զփոխավածառն
եւ ասէ ցնա. Զի՞նչ է այս որ լսեմ, զի գողանաս անձինս յերկրէն
Քանանացւոց ի ծառայութիւն քեզ եւ յաղախնութիւն։ 2 Անկեալ ի
վերայ երեսաց իւրոց փոխավածառն եւ ասէ. Աղաչեմ զքեզ տէր, ոչ
գիտեմ զինչ խաւսիդ։ 3 Եւ նա ասէ. Ուստի՞ է քո պատանեակդ
երրայեցի։ Եւ ասէ փոխավածառն. համայելացիքն եօւն զդա ցիս մինչեւ դարձին այսրէն։ 4 Եւ ոչ հաւատաց նմա այլ հրամայեաց մերկ

սեմփիու   M   + որ էր W

     2 inc] + դարձեալ W ։ որում էր երրայեցի M ։
ուրում] միոյ X   ուրեմն L W   որում K։   երրայեցւոյ]
+ զոր W ։։   թէ] om K S

     3 արդ]   եւ X L ։   արա այժմ K ։   ընդ նմա] M L
om Z   ընդ նոսա X   postդատաստան K S W ։   առ] + ի
նմանէն M   + ի նմանէ X L S W ։   զմանուկն] + ի նմանէ K ։։
շնորհ...է   K S W

     13։1 inc] Z +եւ նորա rel ։   զարթուցեալ K   ուրախացեալ
W ։ ընդ] ի X L ։   բանն K S ։   նորա] Z   om rel ։
հրամայեաց ածել] W B   ած X L   ածէ rel ։   որ] Z L զոր
rel ։   լսեմ] Z K   լսեմս rel ։   գողանան M ։   անձինք
M*   անձն K S W ։։   յաղախնութիւնս X

     2 inc] + յայնժամ X + եւ աոժամայն K + եւ W ։
եւ 1°]   om W ։   ասէ] + ցնա W ։   տէր] + իմ X

     3 քո] քեզ L ։   պատանիդ K S W ։   ասէ փոխ.] Z W նա
ասէ rel ։   ցիս] յիս ի պահ MXL +ի պահեստի K S W

     4 եւ 1°] + պետափրէ W ։   մերկ---ցնա] մերկացուցանել
ցնա եւ շարշարել Z ։   յամառեցաւ X L ։   նա] om X L W ։
ի] առ W ։   ածէք ասէ X L ։   ասէ] + պետափրէ W B ։

looked, she saw me.   2 And she said to her husband concerning the dealer, that he had grown rich through a certain Hebrew youth and men say that by theft they stole him from the land of Canaan.   3 Accordingly, now carry out judgement against him and take the youth for stewardship for yourself, and the God of the Hebrews will bless you, for the grace of heaven is in him.

13:1 Rejoicing at her words, he commanded to bring the dealer and said to him, 'What is this that I hear, that you steal souls from the land of Canaan for male servitude for you and for female servitude?'   2 Falling upon his face the dealer also said, 'I beseech you, lord, I know not what you are saying.' 3 And he said, 'From where is this Hebrew slave of yours?' And the dealer said, 'The Ishmaelites gave him to me until they return again.'   4 And he did not believe him, but ordered him to be tortured naked.

---

   2 inc]   + again W :   through a youth, who possessed a Hebrew M :   certain]   to whom K :   and 2°]   + whom W : men say]   *lit.* they say :   Canaan]   *lit.* of the Canaanites throughout

   3 accordingly]   and X L :   carry out now K : against him]   om Z   against them X :   take]   + from him M X L S W :   youth]   + from him K :   heaven]   *lit.* firmament, cf. Gen. 1:6 *et al.*

   13:1 inc] Z   + and he rel :   rejoicing]   having been aroused K   gladdened W :   her] Z   om rel :   word K S :   commanded to bring] W B   brought X L   brings rel :   souls are stolen M*:   a soul K S W :   females servitudes X

   2 inc]   + then X   + and immediately K   + and W : also]   om W :   said]   + to him W :   lord]   my lord X

   3 of yours]   to you L :   the dealer] Z W   he rel : to me]   + to keep M X L   + for a keeping K S W

   4 he 1°]   Petap're W :   to be---naked]   to undress him and to torture (him)   Z :

տանջել զնա. եւ իբրեւ յամառեաց նա ի նմին բանսն ասէ. Ածէք այր զմանուկն: 5 Եւ իբրեւ տարան զիս երկիր պագի նմա, վասն զի երկրորդ էր զանն նորա փարաւոնի: 6 Եւ զատուցեալ զիս ի նոցանէ ասէ գիս. ծառայ ես եթէ ազատ. եւ ասացի եթե, ծառայ եմ: 7 Եւ ասէ գիս. Ո՛ր ես ծառայ. եւ ասացի եթե համայելացւոցն: 8 Եւ նա ասէ. Զիա՞րդ լինիս նոցա ծառայ. եւ ասացի եթե Յերկրէն Քանանացւոց գնեցին զիս: 9 Եւ ասէ գիս. Սուս ասես. եւ մերկ հրամայեաց տանջել զիս:

14:1 Իսկ Մեմփիու տեսանէր զիս ընդ պատուհանն: 2 Եւ իբրեւ ոչ շրջեցի զբանսն, հրամայեաց զիս դնել ի բանդի մինչեւ եկեսցեն, ասէ, տեարքն իմ: 3 Եւ կինն ասէ գնա. Ապիրատ են դատաստանքդ, զզողացեալդ արգելու՞ս իբրեւ զանիրաւս, որում պարտ է լինել

———

զմանուկն] +եւ նա ասէ մեզ զամենայն W

5 էր] om S : զան՜ն նորա] post փարաւոնի X L : ի
փարաւոնէ M X K S

6 զատոյց M : գիս] om X L

7 գիս] om X : որոյ X L : համայելացւոյն W

8 ասէ] +գիս W : լինիս] ես Z եղեր X W :
գիս] om L

9 սուտ ասես] սուտես K : հրամայեաց մերկ M X L :
հրամայեաց (+եւ W) զիս մերկ տանջել K S W

14:1 մեմփիու Z M S մեփիու L մեմփուի K

2 եւ] Z W om rel : շրջեցի] Z փոխեցի rel :
զբանն S +իմ X L K S W : դնել ի բանդի] Z ի բանդ արկանել rel : ասէ] X Bb om rel: տեարք դորա X

3 դատաստանք W +քո K S W +եւ M +զի X L S
W : զզողացեալդ] X L K S W զզողացեալն Z զզողացեալդ
M : զանիրաւ] զապիրատ X L : որում] արդ X : լինել]
+ապատամբ առն փոխավածանի եւ զդա X +իբրեւ զապիրատ զայն եւ
զդա˚ L : յընդարձակութիւն M ընդարձակութիւն X L ընդ

13:4-14:3 TESTAMENT OF JOSEPH 43

And when he persisted in the same account, he said, 'Bring the youth here!' 5 And when they brought me, I prostrated myself to him because his rank was second to Pharaoh's. 6 And taking me apart from them he said to me, 'Are you a slave or a free man?' And I said, 'I am a slave.' 7 And he said to me, 'Whose slave are you?' And I said, 'The Ishmaelites'.' 8 And he said, 'How did you become their slave?' And I said, 'They bought me from the land of Canaan.' 9 And he said to me, 'You are telling a lie.' And he commanded that I be tortured naked.

14:1 But Memp'iu saw me through the window. 2 And when I did not change these words, he commanded to place me in prison until my masters come, he said. 3 And the woman said to him, 'These judgements are wicked. Will you detain this one who was stolen, like the lawless,

---

bring, he said X L :   he 3°]   Petap'rē W B :   here]
+ and he (will) say everything to us W

    5 his rank] *after* Pharaoh X L :   rank] *or* throne : was] om S

    6 he took me apart M :   to me]   om X L

    7 to me] om X :   Ishmaelite's W

    8 said 1°]   + to me W :   did you become]   are you Z :   me] om L

    9 you---lie]   you lie K :   he---naked (*lit.* naked he commanded to torture me)] Z   he commanded naked to torture me M X L   he commanded (+ also W) me naked to torture K S W

    14:1 Memp'iu] X W   various spelling variants rel : 14:1 b, cf. vs. 3

    2 and] Z W   om rel :   my words X L K W   my word S :   to place me in] Z   to cast me into rel :   his masters X :   he said] X Bb   om rel

    3 these]   your K S W :   and you will M   for you will X L S W :   those who were stolen Z M :   lawless] wicked X L

յընդարձակութեան սպասաւորել քեզ: 4 Վասն զի կամէր կարաւտու-
թեամբ տեսանել զիս. եւ ես ոչ գիտեի յաղագս այսր ամենայնի:
5 Եւ նա ասէ ցմեմփիու. Ո՞չ են աւրէնք առ եգիպտացւոց յառաջագոյն
քան գաստուճել զիրն, առնուլ զայլոյ: 6 Զնոյնն ասաց եւ փոխակա-
ծառն եւ մանուկն եթէ պարտ է լինել նմա ի կապանս. եւ ապա լուեաց
Մեմփիու:

15:1 Եւ յետ քառն եւ չորից աւուրց եկին համայելացիքն, եւ
լուեալ յերկրին Քանանացւոց եթէ Յակոբ սգայ գորդին իւր, եւ ասեն
ցիս. 2 Չի՞ է զի ասացեր զքեն եթէ ծառայ եմ. ապա գիտացաք զքեն
զի որդի ես առն մեծի յերկրէն Քանանացւոց եւ սգայ վասն քո հայր
քո խորգով: 3 Եւ իմ սատակապէս կամեցեալ արտասուել արգելի զիս,

արծակի K S ընդարձակ W + թողուլ եւ X + եւ L W :
սպասաւորել] ծառայել K S W : սպասաւորել---տեսանել (vs 4)]
om M : զքեզ K

    4 գիտեի] եի գիտակ X + թե K +եթե S W +էր
քանն W

    5 նա] այրն W : ցմեմփիու] ed ցմեմփեթիա Z ցմեմ-
փեա M ցմեփիու X L ցմեմփիա S ցմեփփիու K ցմեմփա W :
առ] om K : եգիպտացիսն M S W -ացիս X L : յառաջա-
գոյնք K : քան գատ. զիրն] քաղցրուցանելն X անցուցանել
K : գատուզել զիրն] զգուցանելն M L W ցուցանելն S :
զայլոյ] զայլոց X S + ինչ X L S

    6 զնոյնն---կապանս] om Z : զորյն X : եւ 1°] om
S W : մանուկ նորա X : եթե---կապանս] om X : նմա լինել
W : նմա] om S : կապանս] կամս K : մեմփիու] մեմփեթիու
Z մեփիու X L
    15:1 աւուր Z : յերկրէն M X L K S W : ողբայ Յակոբ K
S W : եւ ասեն ցիս] om L եւ եկին առ իս եւ ասեն W
    2 զի է զի] զիարդ K : զքեն 1°] om Z ցմեզ X Ե աճա--
զքեն 2°] om X L : մեծի] ճզաւրի K S W : եւ 1°] աճա
նա X : ասաց W : հայր քո]ZW om rel ante սգայ W
    3 իմ] om W : կամեցալ W + եւ et ante սատկ. W
post արտասուել K : արտասուել]Z լալ rel + եւ X L K

he who should be at liberty to serve you?' 4 Because, due to desire, she wished to see me and I knew not about all this. 5 And he said to Memp'iu, 'It is not the custom among the Egyptians to take another's property before the proving of the matter.' 6 And he said the same, that it is necessary for both the dealer and the youth to be in bonds. And then Memp'iu was silent.

15:1 And after twenty-four days the Ishmaelites came and, having heard in the land of Canaan that Jacob was mourning his son, they said to me, 2 'Why is it that you said of yourself, "I am a slave."? Behold, we learned about you that you are the son of a great man from the land of Canaan and your father is mourning because of you in sack-cloth.' 3 And, although desiring greatly to weep, I restrained myself

---

he who]   now he X :   be]   + for the rebellious man, the dealer and him X   + like that wicked man and him L :   who should have liberty X L :   free K S W   + to leave and X + and   L W :   to serve---to see (vs 4)]   om M

   4 knew]   was experienced X :   not]   + that K S W + it was the concern W

   5 he]   the man W :   Memp'iu] ed   various spelling variants omn :   among]   of K :   another's]   other people's X S :   proving---matter]   *corrupt* X   passing K demonstration   M L S W

   6 and he---bonds]   om Z :   and 1°]   om S W :   his youth X :   that it is necessary---to be in bonds]   om X : bonds]   will K :   Memp't'iu Z   Mep'iu X L

   15:1 from the land M X L K S W :   Jacob was lamenting K S W :   they said to me]   om L :   they came to me and said W

   2 why is it that]   how K :   of yourself]   om Z   to us X L :   behold---you 1°]   om X L :   great]   powerful K S W :   and]   behold X :   your father] Z W   om rel : mourned W

   3 I desired W :   to weep greatly K :   to weep]   Z to cry rel   + and X L K S   + because of my father and W

զի մի յամաւթ արարից գեղբարսն իմ։ 4 Յայնժամ խորհեին վանատել զիս, զի մի գտայց ի ձեռս նոցա։ 5 Վասն զի երկնչեին ի Յակոբայ, զի մի արասցէ ընդ նոսա վրէժխնդրութիւն վտանկից, զի լսեին զնմանէ եթե մեծ է առաջի Տեառն եւ մարդկան։ 6 Յայնժամ ասէ փոխավանն գնոսա. Արձակեցէք զիս ի դատաստանացն Փոտիփարայ երկրորդի։ 7 Եւ մտեալք առաջի նորա խնդրեին զիս եւ ասեին եթէ, Արծաթոյ գնեցաք զդա, եւ փոխավանն վճարեաց զմեզ։

16:1 Եւ Մեմփիու տապեաց առ այրն իւր զի գնեացէ զիս. Վասն զի լսեմ, ասէ, զի վանոտեն զդա։ 2 Եւ այլ ներքինի դարձեալ առ համայելացի ն տապեաց եւ խնդրէր զիս ի նոցանէ գնել։ 3 Եւ կոչեալ ‹խոհակերապետին› զվանատականսն խնդրէր զիս ի նոցանէ գնոյ, եւ նշանակեաց ներքինին կնոջն եթէ բազում գինս խնդրեն։ 4 Եւ նա ասէ

S +վասն հաւրն իմոյ եւ W

4 խորհուրդ արարին M X L K S W :   զիս] om L :   ի ձեռս նոցա] առ նոսա K S W

5 ի] om X :   ընդ նոսա] postվրէժխնդ. K :   զի 8°] վասն զի K :   տեառն] աստուծոյ S

6 գնոսա փոխավաձ. X L :   ընդ նոսա S W :   փոտիփարի L   պետափրեայ K   պեափրէէ S   պետափրէի W :   երրորդի M   երկրորդէ K   երրորդէ S W   +արքային X

7 մտաք K S   մտին W :   նորա] + եւ K W :   ասէ ցյա K   ասեն ցնա S W :   գնեցէք K :   զփոխավանն վճարեցաք մեք W :   զմեզ] om X L

16:1 մեմփթիու Z մեփիու X L մեմթիու S մեմթայի W : իւր] om M X L :   զիս] + եւ W :   ասէ] om M L K S ante վասն W :   վասն] om K :   գնա M*

2 այլ] այրն W :   դարձեալ] om X L W :   տապեաց] ante դարձեալ K S ante առ M X L W :   գնել] գնոյ M K S W   գնով X   գնոյ---գնոյ (vs 3) om W

3 խոհակերապետին] ed   խոհերապետին Z   խոհապետին M X L K S   +եւ X :   ի նոցանէ] om K S :   ներքին S :

so that I should not put my brothers to shame. 4 Then they planned to sell me so that I might not be found in their hands; 5 because they were afraid of Jacob, lest he take vengeance of punishment upon them; for they had heard concerning him, that he was great before the Lord and men. 6 Then the dealer said to them, 'Free me from the judgements of Potiphar the second.' 7 And, having entered before him, they questioned me and said, 'We bought him for silver, and the dealer paid us.'

16:1 And Memp'iu sent (word) to her husband that he should buy me, 'Because I hear,' she said, 'that they are selling him.' 2 And she sent another eunuch again to the Ishmaelites and sought to buy me from them. 3 And the (chief-cook) having summoned the dealers, asked me from them for a price. And the eunuch indicated to the woman (? his wife) that they were asking a high price. 4 And she said, 'Even

---

4 planned] Z   took counsel rel :   me] om L : in their hands] with them K S W

5 for] because K :   the Lord] God S

6_ to them the dealer X L :   with them S W :   of Petap're K S W :   the second] the third M   corrupt S W + of the king X, cf. 13:5

7 we entered K S   they entered W :   him] + and K W :   he said K   + to him S W :   you bought K :   we paid the dealer W :   paid] or   set free :   us] om X L

16:1 Memp'iu] M K   various spelling variants rel : her] om M X L :   me] + and W :   because] since K : said] om M L K S   before because W

2 another] the husband W :   again] om X L W, cf. Greek vss 2,4 :   to buy] in price M K S W   by price X in price--- a price (vs 3) om W

3 chief-cook] ed   corrupt omn   + and X :   from them] om K S

թեպէտ եւ երկուս մասս ոսկի խնդրեցեն, մի խնայիցես: 5 Եւետ
նոցա վաթսուն դահեկան ընդ իմ, եւ ասացեալ եթէ ութսուն դահեկան
եւու ընդ դորա: 6 Եւ իմ գիտացեալ լուր կացի վասն նորա զի մի
տանջեցի:

17:1 Արդ տեսէք որդեակք քանի ինչ կրեցի զի մի յամաւթ արարից
զեղբարս իմ: 2 Եւ դուք սիրեցէք զիրեարս. 3 Վասն զի ցնծայ
Տէր ընդ յաւժարութիւն սրտից որք հաճին ընդ քարիս: 4 Յորժամ
եկին եղբարք իմ յԵգիպտոս, որպէս եւ գիտեն իսկ եթէ զիարդ դարձուցի
անդրէն զարծաթ նոցա եւ ոչ նախատեցի զնոսա այլ մխիթարեցի: 5
Լսեն աւադիկ ասացեն եթէ
սուտ ինչ խաւսեցայ, այլ եւ զկնի մահուան Յակոբայ սիրեցի զդոսա
եւ զամենայն ինչ զոր եւ հրամայեցին ինձ արարի: 6 Եւ ոչ եւու
նեղել դոցա, մինչեւ ի փոքր իրս, եւ եւու դոցա զամենայն ինչ զոր

բազումա L

4 երկու S W: մասն K S: ոսկւոյ X L post
խնդրեսցեն K S W : խնայէք K S W

5 վաթսում դահեկան] post իմ X: դահեկանս S + զին
W : իմ] + ներքինին W : ասաց X: ընդ 2°] վասն W:
նորա M X L K S

6 գիտացեալ] Z + զայս rel

17:1 տեսէք---զի մի] om L : տեսէք] + թէ K S + եթէ
W post որդեակք իմ K S W : որդեակք] + իմ X K S W + թէ
X : ամաւթ L

2 զմիմեանս X L W

3 ընդ յաւժարութիւն] յաւժարութեամբ M X L : սրտի K
S W : որք] յորժամ K S W: քարիս] իրեարս K S 'միմեանս
W

4 գիտեի K: անդրէն] Z om rel

5 աւադիկ] ահաւադիկ S + եւ X L : ահաւասիկ լսեն
եղբարք իմ W : ասացեն] om W : խաւսին L + ես դարձուցա-
նեն յերեսս իմ W : յակոբայ] հաւր իմոյ X : ինչ զոր եւ]
որ ինչ M զոր ինչ X K S W : եւ 3°] om L : ինձ] Z

16:4-17:6   TESTAMENT OF JOSEPH   49

if they should ask two minas of gold, do not be sparing (of it).'
5 And he gave them sixty drachmae for me and said, 'I gave
eighty drachmae for him.'   6 And I, knowing, was silent for
his sake, lest he be tortured.

    17:1 Now you see, children, how many things I underwent
in order not to put my brothers to shame.   2 And you, love
one another.   3 For the Lord rejoices over the inclination of
hearts which take pleasure in good things.   4 When my brothers
came to Egypt, as they know indeed how, I returned their gold
there and I did not blame them, but forgave (them).   5 Behold,
they hear, let them say if I have spoken any lie! But even
after Jacob's death I loved them and did everything which they
ordered me.   6 And I did not permit to afflict them even in
the smallest matters, and I gave them everything

---

    4 minas] portion K S: do not be sparing] plur. K S W

    5 he]   the eunuch W :   sixty drachmae]   *after* me   X
+ price W

    6 knowing]   Z   + this   rel

    17:1 you---not]   om   L :   see] *after* children K S
W :   my children   X K S W

    3 over]   through M X L :   a heart   K S W :   which]
when   K S W :   good things]   one another   K S W

    4 they know]   I knew   K :   there (*or* again)]   Z   om rel

    5 behold]   + and   X L :   they]   my brothers   W :
let them say]   om   W :   I have spoken]   they speak   L
+ they turn my face aside   W :   Jacob's]   my father's   X :
me]   Z   om rel

    6 I did...permit to afflict]   he gave to have   K :
them 1°]   om   K :   matters]   om   K :   and 2°]   but   X

եւ խնդրեցին, եւ ամենայն ինչ որ եւ թէ էր ի ձեռս իմ, ետու դոցա: 7 Որդիք իմ որդիք դոցա եին եւ ծառայք իմ՝ ծառայք դոցա, անձն իմ՝ անձն դոցա եւ երկիր իմ՝ երկիր դոցա. եւ ամենայն ցաւք դոցա, ցաւք ինձ եին. մի եին մեր ամենեցուն խորհուրդք: 8 Եւ ոչ բարձրացուցի զանձն իմ ի միջի նոցա վասն փառացն իմոց:

18:1 Արդ եթէ եւ դուք ընդ նոյն ճանապարհ գնայցէք, որդեակք իմ, եղ Սադայի փառաւորեսցէ զձեզ եւ բարձրացուսցէ մինչեւ ի վեր: 3 Աղաւասիկ տեսանէք զի զդուստր տերանց իմոց առի կնութեան, եւ հարիւր տաղանդ ոսկւոյ ընդ նմա ետուն ինձ, վասն զի Տէր ետ գնոսա ինձ ի ծառայութիւն: 4 Եւ էր նա գեղեցիկ իբրեւ զծաղիկ եւ գեղեցկագոյն քան զընտիրսն հրայելի, եւ քան զշեւի եւ զյուղայ եւ

```
om rel
         6 ետու նեղել ]  ետ ունել   K :    դոցա 1°]    Z    om K :
փոքր]    +ինչ    X L K :    իրս]    om  K :     եւ 2°]    այլ  X :
որ ինչ   M :     եւ 3°]    om  M S W  :     ամենայն]   զամենայն  X K
S W :    որ]    զոր   S :     եւ թե]   om  X K S W
         7 դոցա 2°]    +եւ   X L    +եին   K S W :    անձն...անձն]
անդ...անդ   Z :     եւ 2°]   om  K S W:    դոցա 4°]   +էր  X L :
ցաւ 2°    X L:    ինձ]   իմ  K S W :    եին ինձ   X L :     մի---
fin]  om  K
         8 զանձն իմ]  Z   զիս rel :     մեջ   X L K S W
   18:1 եթէ]   om  M X L K S W :     եւ]   om  M K S W :    ընդ
նոյն] Z    գնոյն  rel :     ճանապարհս  X L :    իմ ]  +ընդ իս
W :    եղ]   իսրայել   M L   զի եւ իսրայել  X :    եղ սադայի]
եւ ասուած   K S W :    փառաւորեսցէն  Z :     բարձրացուսցէն  Z
M*   +ձեզ  W :    ի վեր ]   յաւիտեան  X L
         3 զի]    որ   X :     առի]     +ի  M L    +ինձ  X    +ինձ ի
K S W :     կնութիւն  M L K W :    ընդ նմա]   post ինձ  K S W :
գնոսա]   գնա   Z K    post ինձ 1°    X S :    ինձ 2° ]  om  M L
         4 նա ]   ասանէթ կին իմ  W :     եւ 2°]   ես եի  W   om  S :
եւ 3°]    +ողջախոհ եւ խոնարհ   W :     եւ 4°]   +քան  K S W :
պահեաց---գեղեցկութեամբ ]  om  S     առաւել գեղեցկագոյն եի քան
գնոսա  W :    յակոբայ ]    հարբ մերոյ  W
```

which they sought and whatever was in my hand I gave to them.
7 Their sons were my sons and my slaves their slaves, my soul their soul and my land their land, and all their pains were pains for me and all our thoughts were one. 8 And I did not exalt myself in their midst because of my glory.

18:1 Therefore, if you too will walk along the same path, my sons, El Shaddai will glorify you and exalt you on high. 3 Behold, you see that I took the daughter of my owners as wife and they gave me a hundred talents of gold with her, because God gave them to me in servitude. 4 And she was beautiful as a flower and more beautiful than the elect ones of Israel and than Levi and Judah and Naphthali.

---

7 their slaves] + and X L *preceded by* were K S W : soul...soul] field...field Z : and 2°] om K S W : land 1°] + was X L : a pain 2° X L : for me] my K S W : and all---one] om K

18:1 if] Z om rel : too] om M K S W : along the same] Z the same rel : paths X L : sons] + with me W : El] Israel M L for also Israel X : El Shaddai] also God K S W : they will glorify Z : they will exalt Z M* + for you W : on high] for ever X L

3 that] who X : took] + for me X K S W : them] him (*or* her) M K : to me] om M L

4 she] Asaneth my wife W : and 2°] I was W om S : and 3°] + modest and humble W : and 4°] + than K S W : she 2°---beauty] om S I was more beautiful than they W :

գնեփթադիմ. պատեաց զինքն գեղեցկութեամբ, վասն զի նման եղէ ես ամենեւին Յակոբայ:

19:1 Արդ լուարուք եւ գտեսին իմ զոր տեսի. 2 Երկոտասան եղշերուս տեսանեի զի արածէին, եւ ի նոցանէ ինն ցրուեցան, բայց երեքն ապրեցան, եւ ի վաղիւն եւ նոքա ցրուեցան: 3 Եւ տեսանեի զի երեք եղշերուքն երեք գառինք լինէին եւ աղաղակեցին առ Տէր, եւ եհան զնոսա ի խաւարէ ի լոյս եւ աճ զնոսա ի տեղի դալարկուտ եւ քրային: 4 Եւ անդ աղաղակեցին առ Տէր մինչեւ ժողովեցան առ նոսա իննեքին եղշերուքն, եւ լինէին նոքա իբրեւ գերկոտասան ոչխար. եւ յետ սակաւ միոյ աճեցին եւ լինէին ի հալոս բազումս: 5 Յետ այսորիկ տեսի եւ աճա երկոտասան գուարակ որ ծծէին զմի կով, որ լի սաստիկ կաթանէն ծով գործէր եւ ըմպէին ի նմանէ երկոտասանեքին

19:1 արդ] + եկայք ամենեքեան W : եւ] om W : իմ] Z om rel : տեսի] + յայնժամ K

2 եղշերուս] եղշիւրս L եղշերուք KSW : տեսանեի] ante երկոտ. W : զի արածէին] որ եմք մեք երկոտասան եղբարքս եւ տեսանեի W : եւ 1°] իսկ MKSW : եւ ի նոցանէ] om L : ցրուեցան 1°---ցրուեցան 2°] om M : ապրեցան] արածէին առ միմեանս W : եւ 3°] om SW

3 երեք 1°] om K : եղշերուքն] եղշիւրքն L: եւ եհան --լոյս] post քրային X : խաւարէն MSW : աճ] եհան L : զնոսա 2°] om L : դալարուտ XK դալարի L

4 ժողովեցան] ցրուեցան K : առ նոսա] om L : եղշիւրքն L եղշերուսն S : ոչխար M : ի] om XLKS W : հալտ M : բազում K

5 եւ աճա] om KSW : գերկոտասան W : գուարակ MXL -ակս KS -ակսն W : որ 1°] om MXL զի KW : ծծէին] ZKS արածէին rel : որ 2°] + եւ K : սաստիկ] + ի M : նմանէ] նոցանէն MK նոցանէ XL: երկոտասան XL : անհամարք K : խաշինք MLS հազարք K

She preserved herself with beauty because I was altogether like Jacob.

19:1 Now hear also my vision which I saw. 2 I saw twelve stags which were pasturing and of them, nine were scattered but three were saved. And on the following day they too were scattered. 3 And I saw that the three stags became three lambs and they cried out to the Lord and he brought them forth out of darkness into light and he brought them to a green and watered place. 4 And there they cried out to the Lord until the nine stags were gathered to them and they became like twelve sheep, and after a little they increased and became many flocks. 5 After this I saw and, behold, twelve bulls which were sucking the one cow which, through the vast amount of her milk, was making a sea. And the twelve flocks

---

Jacob] + my father W

    19:1 now] + come all W : also] om W : my] Z om rel : I saw] + then K

    2 stags] horns L : which were pasturing] which are we twelve brothers and I saw W : and 1°] but M K S W : and of them] om L : scattered 1°---scattered 2°] om M : were saved] pastured with one another W : too] om S W

    3 three 1°] om K : stags] horns L : and he brought 1°---light] *after* place X : brought 2°] brought forth L : them 2°] om L

    4 stags] horns L : were gathered] were scattered K : to them] om L : flock M

    5 and behold] om K S W : which] so that they K W : sucking] Z K S pasturing rel : which 2°] + also K :

ՀՏԱԿ ՅՈՎՍԵՓԱՅ 19:5-12

հալոքն եւ անհամար խաշինքն: 6 Եւ չորրորդ զուարակին բարձրաց-
եալ եղջերքն մինչեւ յերկինս, եւ եղեն իբրեւ զպարիսպ հալտիցն,
եւ ի մէջ եղջերացն ծաղկեաց այլ եղջեւր: 7 Եւ տեսանեի որթ որ
թե երկոտասան անգամ պատեր զնովաւ, եւ եղեւ զուարակացն բոլորովին
յաւզնականութիւն: 8 Եւ տեսի ի մէջ եղջերացն կոյս որ ունէր
արկանելի ծամանալուխտ, եւ ի նմանէ ելանէր զառն. եւ յաշմէ կող-
մանէ նորա յարձակէին ամենայն գազանք եւ ամենայն սողունք. եւ
յաղթեաց զնոսա զառնն եւ կորոյս զնոսա: 9 Եւ ինդացին յաղագս
նորա զուարակքն եւ կովն եւ երեքեան եղջիւրքն եւ ցնծային հանդերձ
նովաւ: 10 Եւ այսմ պարտ է լինել ի ժամանակի իւրում: 11 Եւ
դուք որդեակք իմ, պատուեցէք զշեւի եւ զՅուդայ, զի ի նոցանէ
ծագեսցէ ձեզ փրկութիւն իսրայելի: 12 Վասն զի թագաւորութիւնս

                6 բարձրացան M X L K S W :   մէջ] + երկուց   M X L
K S W :   ծագեաց   X L
                7 տեսանէ L :   որթ որ թե]   որթս   X   որդ   L   որ
թուէր K   որ թիւ էր W :   թե] om M S :   անգամ] om X
+ որ   X :   պատեին   X :   պատեր զնովաւ]   պատերազմաք K :
զնքպաք M X L S W :   եղեն   X :   բոլորովին] բոլոր ի մի   M
                8 կոյս] + մի   X :   արկանելիս   M X L   om   K   + ի
S :   ծանծանալուխս W :   արձակէին K S W :   զնոսա] Z   նոցա
rel
                9 խնդացին]   խնդրեցին   L :   եւ կովն եւ]   երկուքն K
կունքն   S W :   երեք   M K S W   om   X L :   եղջիւրքն]
եղջերուքն   M X   եղջերացն   K S W :   եւ 4°]   om   M X L K S W
                10 այսմ]   այս   K   + ամենայնի   X
                11 ձեզ] Z M   om   rel
                12 Թագաւորութեանս   X :   իմ] om K S W :   է]   om
X L :   վախճանեցցի] K S W   եղիցի ի վախճանի Z   եղիցի վախճան

and the innumerable herds were drinking from it. 6 And the horns of the fourth bull were elevated up to the heavens and became like a wall for the flocks and another horn flowered between the horns. 7 And I saw a calf which circled it twelve times and became an aid to the bulls altogether. 8 And I saw among the horns a virgin who had a many-coloured garment and from her a lamb went forth. And from its right side all wild beasts and creeping things attacked and the lamb overcame them and destroyed them. 9 And the bulls and the cow and the three horns were glad because of it and rejoiced with it. 10 This must take place in its time. 11 And you, my children, honour Levi and Judah, for from them the salvation of Israel shall shine forth for you. 12 Because my kingdom

---

herds] thousands K :   from it]   from them M X L K

    6 were elevated] *lit.* being elevated Z   were elevated rel :   flowered]   sprang up X L :   the 5°]   + two M X L K S W

    7 he saw L :   a calf which]   calves X   which seemed K   which number was W :   circled (plur.) X :   circled it]   by wars K :   it]   them M X L S W :   times]   om X + which X :   became (plur.) X :   altogether]   all in one M

    8 a 1°]   a certain X :   garments M X L   om K + to S

    9 and the cow and]   the two K   *corrupt* S W :   the three]   three M K S W   om X L :   horns]   stags M X of the horns K S W :   were glad]   sought L :   and 4°] om M X L K S W

    10 this]   + all X

    11 for you]   Z M   om rel

    12 to my X :   my]   om K S W :

իմ որ է ի միջի ձերում, վախճանեցցի իբրեւ զտաղաւար մրգապահաց, որ ոչ երեւեսցի զկնի ամարայնոյ։

20։1 Գիտեմ զի եգիպտացիքս յետ իմ ներդիցեն զձեզ, այլ Աստուած արասցէ վրէժխնդրութիւն ընդ նոսա եւ տարցի զձեզ ի խոստումն հարցն ձերոց։ 2 Բայց տարջիք զոսկերս իմ անդրէն ընդ ձեզ։ 3 Եւ գձելփա մայր ձեր հանջիք, եւ մեռծ ի Բալլա առ Չիարշաւանսն եւ առ Հոքբէլ մայր իմ, անդր դիջիք զնա։ 4 Եւ պարգեալ զոտս իւր վախ- ճանեցաւ։ 5 Եւ սգաց զնա ամենայն իսրայէլ եւ ամենայն եգիպտոս սուզ մեծ։

---

rel ։ զտաղաւարի X։ մրգապահ L։ ամարայնոյ] ի մարան K ի մարմնի W

20։1 յետ իմ] post զձեզ K S ։ իմ] իմոյս ելանելոյ X իմոյ ելանելոյ L ։ ընդ] ի M X L K S W ։ հաւրն ձերում K

2 անդրէն] Z om rel

3 գեղփա M L W գեղբարս K գեղբարսն S ։ մայր 1°] om K S ։ հանեք X հանգուսջիք K S ։ եւ մեռձ--- ձիարշաւանսն] Z om rel ։ եւ առ---մայր իմ] om Z ։ եւ 3°] om M + դրեք X ։ հոաբել] ռաքուէլ M բեոս K բեոսն S ։ քոյրս W + եւ առ K S + եւ W ։ մայրս K S W ։ իմ] om K S ։ անդր] Z om rel ։ դիջիք զնա] om X ։ զնա] om L

4 inc] + եւ յետ այսորիկ W ։ պարգեալ] պարգեաց K S W ։ իւր] Z K S W om rel + եւ K S W ։ վախճանեցաւ] + յովսէփ ծ. եւ ժ. ամաց X

5 սգաց] Z ելաց M L W լացին X K S ։ եգիպտոս] + էառ M + առ L

19:12-20:5   TESTAMENT OF JOSEPH   57

which is in your midst will come to an end, like a gardener's hut which will not be seen after the summer.

20:1 I know that after me the Egyptians will afflict you, but God will take vengeance upon them and will bring you to that promised to your fathers. 2 But bring my bones from there with you. 3 And bring forth Zilpah your mother and, close to Bilhah, by the Hippodrome and by Rachel my mother, there place her." 4 And stretching out his feet, he died. 5 And all Israel mourned him and all Egypt, with great mourning.

---

is]   om   X L :   will come to an end]   K S W   will be at the end   Z M   will be an end   X L :   the summer]   in war K   in body   W

   20:1   after me]   *after* you   K S :   me]   my going forth X L :   your father   K

   2 from there]   Z   om rel

   3 bring forth]   lay to rest   K S :   Zilpah your mother] your brothers   K S :   and close---Hippodrome]   Z   om rel : and by---mother 2°]   om   Z :   and 3°]   om   M   + place   X : Rachel]   Raguel   M   sister   K S W   + and by   K S   + and W :   my]   om   K S :   there]   Z   om rel :   place her] om   X :   her]   om   L

   4 inc]   + and after this   W :   he stretched   K S W : his]   Z K S W   om rel   + and K S W :   he]   Joseph...at 110 years   X

   5 mourned]   Z   bewailed   rel :   with]   took on   M L